Slime and Punishment
Life's Outtakes - Year 10

52 Humorous and Inspirational Short Stories

By
Daris Howard

A collection of stories, humorous anecdotes, thoughts, and tidbits of wisdom from the popular newspaper column.

Publishing Inspiration

Slime and Punishment

Life's Outtakes - Year 10

52 Humorous and Inspirational Short Stories

By

Daris W. Howard

A collection of stories, humorous anecdotes, thoughts, and tidbits of wisdom from the newspaper column *Life's Outtakes*.

ISBN-10: 1629860174
ISBN-13: 978-1629860176

www.publishinginspiration.com

Publishing Date: July 3, 2017

Publishing Inspiration LLC

Table of Contents

Dear Reader,

People often ask me if my stories are true. Though I must admit that I tend to take a bit of literary license in my writing, each story is based on an actual event. Sometimes the stranger stories are the ones that are stretched the least. As people often say, truth is stranger than fiction.

I also want to note that some of the names have been changed to protect the anonymity of the individuals.

Daris Howard

Toothaches and Painkillers

✦

Years ago, about the time Russia was opening up more to western tourists, three of my colleagues from the University decided to take a few weeks of their summer and travel there. They didn't have any itinerary; instead, they decided to just go and hope for the best. Upon their return, I asked Loren about their trip.

"We had lots of great times and new adventures," was the reply. "We rented a little car that we drove around. I think we had someone following us for quite a while, but eventually they must have decided we were harmless. That was when we decided we would go farther out into the country to see how the common people lived."

"I bet that was fun," I said.

"It was kind of fun," Loren said. "But the farther we got away from the main cities, the fewer people spoke English, and none of us spoke Russian. We were able to get along for quite a while, using hand gestures to help people understand what we wanted. We were able to buy food, find places to stay and buy the other things we needed. But then, one evening when we were eating dinner, Bert cracked a tooth.

"It hurt him a lot, but he said he could manage until we arrived back in the United States. It got worse quickly, though, and in just a couple of days, he was in so much pain that he couldn't eat anything. We finally decided we needed to find a dentist and get his tooth taken care of.

"We tried to ask people where we could find a dentist. We pointed at our mouths, and they brought food to sell to us. We pointed at our teeth, and they provided the worst looking toothbrushes for us to buy, along with terrible smelling pastes and powders that we figured must have been some kind of toothpaste. We pointed at Bert and then at our teeth and made groaning sounds, and they must have figured that we were sick because then they tried to avoid us.

"Finally, we arrived at a town that was a little bigger. We went to a store there and asked if anyone could speak English. The store owner brought out his college-age son. By speaking slowly, we were able to make him understand what we wanted. He said there was a dentist in the town and that he would take us there.

"He rode with us, giving directions until we pulled up in front of a shabby little building. It didn't look all that sanitary, and Bert would have changed his mind if he hadn't been in so much pain.

"We entered the building. The room was only about ten feet by ten feet, with one hard wooden chair and a small table beside it. The dentist spoke simple English he had learned in college. He said we would have to pay extra since we didn't have an appointment and would be taking time away from his scheduled patients. The only other person there was his assistant, but we paid the price.

"Bert sat in the chair, and the dentist looked at his tooth. The dentist said, 'Me no able to fix. Must pull.' With that, he reached over and grabbed a big set of pinchers from the table.

"The look on Bert's face was priceless. He stopped the dentist. 'Don't you have some painkiller you can give me?' he asked.

"The dentist nodded. 'We have something to handle pain, but cost extra.' We again paid the money. The dentist then turned to the large woman who was his assistant. 'Helga, handle pain!' The woman grabbed Bert in a headlock and held him where the dentist could get at him. The dentist reached into Bert's mouth and jerked out the tooth.'"

"I bet he was glad to have that over with," I said.

Loren nodded. "Bert said he was just glad the dentist got the tooth on the first try. He said the painkiller was strong enough he about passed out, and he didn't think he could stand a second dose."

When the Honeymoon Is Over

✦

My wife, Donna, grew up in Los Angeles, and I was afraid my rural upbringing would scare her off. But she was one of the few girls I met who was not afraid to try new things. I, too, was always willing to try new things, and I found myself stepping out of my comfort zone many times as we visited her family.

Donna and I both learned a lot from each other, and as time went on, we married. There were things about city life that were tough for me, but it was Donna who ended up with the biggest challenge.

The night after we were married, we had a reception and left to spend two weeks on our honeymoon. We traveled to meet family members who were scattered across the United States. We arrived back at my parents' home on a Thursday evening with plans to spend Friday setting up for an open house that would be on Saturday.

I was one of the youngest boys of my family, so my father had sold the cows and rented out the farm when I left home. But he still kept about a dozen young heifers.

The night we arrived, he came to talk to me. "Daris," he said, "the heifers were all bred about the same time, and if my calculations are correct, I think they should be calving anytime. Would you mind checking on them for me tomorrow?"

I told him I would, and the next morning right after breakfast, I walked out to the pasture. I hadn't gone very far when I came across one of the heifers. She was lying on her side trying to birth a calf, but it was stuck. As I approached her, even in her extreme pain, she rose to her feet and moved to keep her distance from me. I knew I had to get her in the barn where I could help her, or she would die. I also knew I couldn't herd her there alone, so I asked Donna to help me.

Despite the heifer's belligerence, Donna and I finally had the cow locked in a stall in the barn. Then came the big learning experience for Donna.

The only parts of the calf that showed were one hoof, the nose, and a swollen tongue. I figured the calf was probably dead, but I still needed to work quickly to save the mother.

I tied some twine to the leg that was visible and pushed it and the head back in. I asked Donna to hold the cow's tail out of the way, and then I reached in, holding another piece of twine in my hand. When I did, the cow strained against me, crushing my arm. This was something I had done hundreds of times while I was growing up, but it was new to Donna, and she looked on wide-eyed.

I was finally able to feel the second hoof and eventually managed to slip a loop of the twine around it. I worked that hoof up with the other one, and then I pulled. By that time I was exhausted, but it was exhilarating to see the calf slide out into the straw. And what was more exciting, even though his nose and tongue were so swollen he could hardly breathe, he was still alive.

We put the mother and her baby into a nice, clean pen and went to check on the other heifers. We found three more of them in desperate need of help. To our amazement, all of the calves lived, and soon each cow had a baby nursing at her side. By then it was evening, and we had neither eaten lunch nor prepared anything for the reception.

After we had finished, washed, and sat down to dinner, I told my dad about our day.

He laughed and said, "There's nothing like baptism by fire into ranching life for your wife."

Her laughter joined his when he turned to her and said, "But it's too late to back out now because you're already hitched!"

The Color of Things

My friend, Nathan, is an electrician at the university where I work. He put in long hours recently because the campus was finishing a new natural gas heating facility to replace the old coal-fired one. It is huge, and the equipment inside warms every building on campus with heat to spare.

To use the surplus heat, turbines were installed that generate enough electricity for most of the campus. It is new and innovative, but it also required a new electrical grid, new wiring, and new lines all over campus.

That is where my friend came into the picture. Being an electrician, he was responsible for a lot of the new wiring. Since it was more than he could handle alone, ads were posted for two students with skills in that area to work under his direction.

Two young men were hired, and Nathan parceled out work to each of them according to their abilities. As their work demonstrated that they knew what they were doing, he gave them more and more responsibilities.

The project was winding to a close after months of hard work, and they had to replace one last underground wire to the final building. Nathan took his equipment and went to the area where they needed to lay the electric cable. He located the old wire and used red spray paint to mark a line above it on the grass. He then assigned the two young men to take the trencher, which looked like a giant, mobile chainsaw, and cut the trench. After an hour or so, the young men came back.

"We can't find the line you marked," one of them said.

"I'm sure I marked it as well as possible," Nathan replied. "Are you positive you are in the right place?"

The young men told him which lawn they were on. It seemed to be right, but Nathan decided he had better check. They certainly didn't need a trench cut across the wrong lawn. That had happened before, and the landscape person who had to replace the sprinklers was not happy.

Nathan was just heading out with the two young men when an older electrician, who also worked there, stopped him.

"Let me go with them," he said. "You have plenty to do."

Nathan thanked him, and the older man left with the two young men. About fifteen minutes later he returned.

"Did you show them where I marked the line?" Nathan asked.

The old man nodded. "I went right to it. It was obvious. I showed them one of your marks and left them to it."

A little while later, Nathan finished up the work he was doing and decided he had better check to see how the trench was coming along. To his dismay, he found it had been cut across his well-marked line at a ninety-degree angle, destroying much of a formerly beautiful lawn.

Nathan stopped them. "What the devil are you doing? You are supposed to follow the line I marked."

The young man running the machine hung his head. "I'm sorry, Nathan. I couldn't see it, so I just guessed where it was."

Nathan took a deep breath to calm himself even as he spoke. "What do you mean you couldn't see it? It's clearly marked."

"I'm color blind," the young man said. "Red and green look the same to me."

The other young man gasped. "You're color blind? So am I."

"Why didn't you tell me?" Nathan asked.

The young men shrugged sheepishly.

Then Nathan thought of something else that made him shudder. These two color blind young men had been doing color-coded wiring in the buildings all summer.

Something to Sit On

✦

It was a big event in the small Wyoming town. They were
building a new church building, a magnificent structure set high on a
hill, and it would serve the needs of the people for multiple counties.
For the groundbreaking ceremony of this historical building, people
from all over the state were gathering to participate.

Top church leaders were going to officiate, and lots of
dignitaries would be there as well: mayors and councilmen of various
towns were invited, along with sheriffs, county commissioners, and
anyone else of any influence. Even the governor of the state was going
to be there, along with many state legislators. Every person that
wanted to attend, no matter their age or their faith, was invited.

Because the groundbreaking was expected to draw thousands of
people, committees were formed to get the word out and arrange
accommodations for the expected crowd. Porta-potties were brought
into the open field near where the church building was to be built.
Water coolers were borrowed from anyone who had one to provide
cool water for the crowd on that hot summer day.

Every available chair was borrowed from schools, churches,
and businesses. But as the committee added up the number of chairs
that had been promised, they knew it was going to be insufficient for
the expected crowd. They resorted to relying on many attendees
bringing their own chairs.

Getting out the information for people to bring their own chairs
was then turned over to the publicity committee. They published
articles in every newspaper in the area, did interviews on every radio
station, and even made sure every news channel carried
announcements about the event. And with each article, interview, or

news announcement, they were certain to mention that the meeting might be long and seating would be limited.

"Bring anything and everything you have to sit on," they advised. "And if you have extra, please bring extra."

The day before the big event, the committee enlisted the young people of the valley to round up all of the promised chairs. These were lined up on the field in nice, uniform rows. When the last of the chairs was set up, the committee counted them and found they had even fewer than they had hoped for. There was only enough for about half of the expected crowd. There was nothing they could do about it; they would simply have to hope that word had gotten out and that people would bring something to sit on.

As the crowd began to arrive, the chairs that were already set up filled quickly with those who wanted to have front-row seats. Many people did bring additional chairs, which they set up around the perimeter, but this added another problem. The farther away people set up chairs, the less they were able to see of the proceedings.

And then something happened that the committee hadn't expected. What people brought to sit on were horses. People rode them into town or brought them in trailers. And it wasn't just a few. They came by the ones and twos and then by the dozens. By the time the meeting was to proceed, the whole gathering was encircled by scores of people sitting on horses, giving a great view over the top of the crowd to each mounted person.

As the meeting time neared, the committee chairman apologized to the head church leader. "We really didn't expect to have people bring horses."

The church leader just laughed. "Your announcement did say to bring anything they had to sit on. What's better than a horse?"

We Are Family

✦

I was only twenty-five when I was hired to teach in the Math and Computer Science Department of a private, religious junior college. Our department has grown over the years, and we have since become a university, but there has always been a strong camaraderie and concern for each other's welfare. I knew that if I ever had a child admitted to the hospital, or had any other kind of challenge, I could always expect phone calls and visits from the department members.

Dave, one of the more senior members of the department, always said, "We are family." I didn't realize how significant this was until a particular event that occurred a few years after my hire.

Gordon, who was in his early fifties when I was hired, was one of the members of our department who had been there the longest, despite his relatively young age. I had only been there three years when he approached me.

"Daris," he said, "I would like you to take over heading the computer part of our department."

Gordon was not only my mentor, but he was also a good friend. He was one of the most brilliant men I had ever known. He was an incredible teacher and an extremely skilled programmer. He loved his students. He loved learning the new technology. And, in short, he loved heading the computer science part of the department. That he should ask me to take over came as a big surprise.

"Is everything all right, Gordon?" I asked.

He nodded. "I have just felt a little tired and thought it was time to let someone younger take some of the load. I'll continue to work with you and deal with the parts I want to."

I agreed to the new workload and started taking on the challenges of maintaining our computer lab, hiring tutors, and reviewing options for all new equipment. But I never made any major decisions without first passing them by him for his approval.

But as his energy continued to diminish, we all grew increasingly concerned, as did his wife. It took all of us to convince him to go to a doctor to see if anything was wrong. And indeed there was—he had liver cancer.

That is when I truly learned what good people I worked with. Gordon felt he could do chemotherapy and still teach. Besides, he needed to continue working to keep his insurance. But we were only a few weeks into the semester when Gordon no longer had the energy to even get out of bed. That is when the more senior members of our department called a meeting.

"What can we do to help Gordon?" Dave asked.

"Would the university allow us to teach his classes in his stead and let him have the pay and keep his insurance?" I asked.

The department chairman nodded. "As long as they are taught, it doesn't make any difference who does the work."

We immediately divided up his classes. I taught his computer classes and others taught his math classes.

But it didn't stop there. Members of our department continued to check on Gordon to see what he needed. As he grew weaker, we all asked what more we could do. Gordon's sweet wife was very independent, but she did finally let us help. Gordon could not shave himself any longer, and with the challenges she faced, she had no time to mow the lawn or take care of the yard.

I took on the yard assignment. I asked for volunteers from the computer science students. Gordon was well loved, and each week at the appointed hour, dozens of students showed up with rakes, shovels, and all sorts of gardening tools. We mowed, trimmed, and beautified his yard.

But what touched my heart even more was watching the older men of our department kindly and selflessly alternating days visiting Gordon to help him shave and take care of his physical needs.

At Gordon's funeral, his wife rented a limousine and asked me to drive it for the members of our department to act as the pallbearers.

As I drove, hardly able to see for the tears in my eyes, I looked in my rear view mirror at the wonderful people I worked with and remembered Dave's words.

We are family.

Student Communications (2015)

✦

Most of my college students are bright, hard-working, and fun to teach. But each semester I get interesting letters, emails, phone calls, and other correspondence from a select few. I save these and, occasionally, I compile them into a column. I don't think any of these comments need any explanation, other than to say that I changed or removed any names for anonymity. Also, I pared a few of them down a bit.

***

Professor Howard, last week I had the chapters 2 and 3 practice exam completed in class on the appointed day and ready to go over with my group. However, yesterday, when it was actually due, it was nowhere to be found. After making the sad assumption that I had thrown it away by accident, today I came across it in my laundry basket, of all places! If it is possible for me to receive credit for this assignment, even partial credit, that would be greatly appreciated.

***

Hey, Professor Howard, for some reason I thought that the test didn't close till Saturday, so I went in to take it at about one o'clock, and the guy told me it closed yesterday. I was wondering if I could somehow take it for partial credit. I studied really hard for it, even skipping your class the last couple of class days to spend more time studying. I just don't know how I didn't know that it closed Friday.

***

Professor Howard, I didn't have a chance to do the homework before it was due, and now when I try to go in and do it, it won't let me. Can you tell me why?

***

I was taking the 5B quiz after I read the section. Now, you may not believe me, but I read the whole section. I was taking the quiz and didn't recognize anything on it. I checked the answers in the back of the book like you said we could, and the multiple choice answers were mostly different than mine. Well, I reread the section, trying to understand what the quiz was talking about, but it didn't help. I finally just changed all of my answers to the ones in the back of the book and pressed submit. I got a 27%! Then I realized I was reading the 5C quiz, not the 5B quiz. That was a pretty smart move by me—not. Is there any way that I could retake this quiz? If not, I learned my lesson to make sure the answers that I am checking with are the same as the quiz I am taking.

***

Professor Howard, you have probably noticed that my grades for this semester are horrible. I have been lazy, skipped class, and I haven't done most of the homework. But I want you to know that I plan to turn my life around 360 degrees from here on.

***

Professor Howard, I know you told us that we should know the math concepts and not just how to do the mechanics of the problems, but I think that is stupid. Math was discovered thousands of years ago and hasn't had anything new for a long time, so all we should need to do is learn the way people have decided it should be done.

***

(A conversation between two of my students before class.)

Student 1: Did you work problem 7 on the homework?
Student 2: Yes.
Student 1: I read it and considered it, but the more I thought about it, the less I understood it. What should I do?
Student 2: Obviously, you need to quit thinking about it before you don't understand anything at all.

Ticked-Off Kickoff

David, an old high school friend, recently sat by me at a football game. After we watched the opening kickoff, he turned to me and asked, "How did you end up becoming the kick-off person for our high school team? That seems unusual for a lineman."

I smiled as I remembered Tim, our kickoff man. He would often yell over to us, "Hey, any of you losers want to challenge me in kicking the football?"

Tim knew he was good and he loved to show off, humiliating anyone who would take his challenge. Some of the backs tried, but their kicks never even made it to the twenty-yard line. Tim's, on the other hand, always dropped at about the one-yard line.

The back coach stormed over, shaking a finger at Tim. "You quit bugging my players. They have a job to do, and it isn't kicking the ball."

Tim laughed. "Especially since they aren't that good at it, huh?"

The back coach frowned as he herded his young men back to their assignments. As much as Tim mocked the backs, he liked to mock us linemen even more.

Soon he came trotting over to where we were smashing the tackling dummies.

"Hey, any of you guys want to challenge me and see how far you can kick the ball?"

Our line coach, Coach B, yelled, "Get lost! They have more important things to do!"

"Like pound themselves against a bunch of tackle dummies?" Tim asked. "Sometimes it's hard to know which ones the dummies are."

As Tim headed back to his kicking practice, Coach B mumbled, "I feel like showing him who the dummy is."

Our head coach, Coach M, put his hand on Coach B's shoulder. "Just ignore him. We need him. He's one of the best kickers in the state."

"And, unfortunately, he knows it," Coach B replied.

The game day came, and we arrived early to warm up. After a few calisthenics, Coach B looked for a football to use in some fumble drills. Not finding one, he turned to me.

"Howard, run down to the end of the field and get us a football."

I ran all the way and grabbed one out of the bag. When I turned back around, some of the guys started yelling for me to throw it to them. Instead, I kicked it. It not only sailed the full distance to them, but went a good thirty yards beyond. Coach B just stood staring at me as I ran back to the warm up.

"Did you actually kick that from clear down in the end zone?" he asked.

He had seen me do it, so I wasn't sure why he was asking. I just shrugged and nodded.

"How did you learn to kick like that?" he asked.

"I don't know," I replied. "I guess it comes from kicking a ball out in the pasture while I herded cows."

A sly smile crept across his face. "Do you think you could kick that way from a tee?"

"I don't know," I replied. "I've never tried."

"Well, it's time you did."

Coach B sent me over to where Tim was still mocking and challenging people. Coach B, meanwhile, went to "casually" make sure Coach M was watching.

Tim smiled when I accepted his challenge. He said, "Let me show you how it's done."

He put the ball on the tee, backed his steps off, ran up, and kicked it. The ball sailed through the air, dropping a yard short of the goal line.

He continued to grin as I placed the ball on the tee. I backed up, measuring my steps like I had many times at home, then ran and kicked the ball. It sailed through the air, barely under the crossbar on the goal posts, hit beyond the end of the end zone, and bounced over the fence at the edge of the field.

Suddenly Coach B and Coach M were there.

"Who in the world kicked that ball?" Coach M asked. Tim stood in shock as those standing nearby pointed at me.

"Well, Howard," Coach M said, "I think our team has a new kicker."

As David waited for me to answer how I became the kicker, I shrugged. "Just luck, I guess."

Who's the Boss?

✦

Our old horse died, and my wife and children wanted another one. I finally agreed, but I insisted that we find one that was gentle but not too old. My wife searched, and eventually she informed me that she had found the perfect one.

At the horse farm, the owner took us to a pasture full of horses. She pointed out a beautiful gelding. "That's the horse. He is really gentle."

"Why are you selling him?" I asked.

"Because he has no fire," she replied.

"What do you mean?"

"I'm a barrel racer in the rodeo," she answered. "Some horses have such a competitive spirit that they will work to win with or without their rider. But competition is not a big deal to this horse. In fact, he's the low man in the herd. He lets all of the other horses push him around."

I could see what she meant. The other horses would nip at him, and he would immediately back off, not wanting to cause trouble. Still, I could tell he was irritated at being at the bottom of the pecking order.

We bought the horse and named him Caspian. I put him in the pasture with our old cow, Leah. He ran around the pasture for a brief time and then approached Leah cautiously. She backed away, and Caspian seemed surprised. None of the horses backed away from him. Suddenly, he seemed to see a chance to assert himself at the top of the pecking order. He moved aggressively toward Leah, and she responded by turning and running. He chased her.

I knew this would not be good for her milk production, so I tied him up and built a fence to split the pasture. The fence kept them apart, but if Caspian ever got in with Leah, he would chase her to make sure she remembered that he was in charge.

When the time approached for Leah to give birth, we realized we needed another cow. Our youngest daughter could drink raw milk but would break out in a rash from any that was pasteurized. I bought a young cow, whom we named Coco. The farmer I bought her from left me with a warning that Coco was probably coming into heat.

I had no sooner put Coco into the pasture with Leah than Caspian was trying to find a way through the fence. He seemed determined to make sure Coco knew he was the boss. As I watched, I saw him search the fence line. Eventually, he found a gate with a loose latch.

Caspian popped the gate open and took off at full speed toward Coco. But Coco didn't run away. In fact, she ran toward him. I realized she must be in heat, but I was confused as to why she would chase the horse. Then it dawned on me—she had always been artificially bred before, so she had never seen a bull. Caspian was probably as bull-like as anything Coco's cow brain could imagine, so she was, of course, instantly in love.

Caspian realized something was wrong and slid to a stop, just in time for Coco to jump on him. Suddenly, Caspian realized he wanted nothing to do with this lovesick cow. He fled back toward his pasture. But much to his chagrin, he found the gate had relatched, and he was trapped with this crazy cow.

She chased him, and he whinnied for help. Coco cornered Caspian and jumped all over him until he was able to break free and run for it. Coco continued to chase, corner, and jump on him for some time until I finally took pity on him and went to his rescue.

I unlatched the gate and let Caspian back into his pasture. He ran to the farthest side, trembling from the emotional trauma he had suffered, while Coco paced the fence line trying to get to him.

Returning to the house, I told my wife that I didn't think we would have to worry about Caspian chasing the cows anymore. I was right, but we did have to endure Coco's lovesick mooing for a few sleepless nights.

A Rule of Thumb: Timing is Everything

Derek, a friend of mine, had lost half of his thumb to a power saw while building kitchen cabinets. Despite this setback, I never once saw him discouraged, even during the days of his recovery. He always found a way to keep his sense of humor.

One day he agreed to let my scout troop use his wood shop to build our sled for the Klondike Derby. The boys agreed that, in exchange, they would help clean his shop.

Derek spent quite a bit of time talking to the boys about safety and was insistent that they follow the rules to a T. But never once did he talk about his thumb. I had assumed he would use the accident as a powerful example of what not to do, but I decided he must be embarrassed about it because he never mentioned it.

Even with all of Derek's discussion of safety, it was all we could do to keep the eighteen boys out of trouble. Each time we worked on the sled, there were more than a few of them that went home covered with wood glue or wearing clothes painted a different color than when they came. But the boys worked hard, enthusiastic about the job at hand, and with Derek's wonderful tools and great direction we built a beautiful, sleek sled. It took us a few scout meetings to finish the job, but when it was completed, the boys were proud of their work.

When it came time to clean, their enthusiasm waned a bit. I told them that with the twenty of us, we should be able to make short work of it. Derek directed the cleaning, and I worked alongside the boys since that was the only way to keep them on task.

We loaded the garbage into Derek's old pickup truck. The handle on the tailgate was broken, and we had to use a pair of pliers to open it, but the truck was large and held a lot. After two trips to the landfill, the shop was finally looking more orderly.

While Derek and I were loading the last of the garbage into his truck, the boys played a game of steal the flag. Then the subject of his injured thumb came up.

"I am just a bit curious," I said. "I thought when you talked to the boys about safety that you might mention your accident."

Derek laughed. "Actually, I save that until just the right moment. Timing is everything."

"Like what?" I asked.

"You'll see," he replied.

It wasn't too long before the game of steal the flag ended and the boys came over.

"Hey, Gordy," Derek said to the oldest scout, "would you mind closing the tailgate of my pickup while I hold the garbage out of the way?"

Gordy nodded and slammed the tailgate shut. The instant it latched, Derek put his cut thumb into the crack at the edge and started to scream, "You caught my thumb!" He continued to scream as the boys rushed around, knocking each other down trying to find some pliers to open the tailgate while I almost suffocated myself trying to conceal my laughter.

The more the boys tried to hurry, the more chaotic their scramble became. They eventually found pliers, dropping them multiple times in their anxiety. But finally the tailgate popped open, and Derek pulled his thumb out and held it up. The boys shuddered, thinking they had cut it off. Then one of them asked suspiciously, "Why isn't it bleeding?"

Derek started to laugh. "You know, come to think of it, that's the one I cut the end off of a few years ago with the table saw."

Although clearly relieved, the boys looked sheepish as they realized they'd been had.

Laughing, Derek turned to me and said, "Timing truly is everything."

An Ounce of Understanding

I looked at my class roll and turned to Colleen. "Colleen, it's your turn for the presentation today."

She looked up, anger showing on her face. "I don't want to do a stupid presentation! I don't know why you expect something dumb like that anyway! You can take it and shove it, as far as I'm concerned!"

She continued her tirade at me for a few minutes while the other students stared. She said she hated me, the class, the university, and apparently everything else she could think of. I felt anger surge through me briefly, but it was quickly displaced by a memory of when, as a young professor in a similar situation, a colleague helped me realize that an ounce of understanding would negate pounds of regret.

I took a deep breath, but another student spoke before I could. "Look, you!" she said to Colleen. "You have no right to speak that way!"

Colleen turned angrily to her, and I could see she planned to verbally assault the other student, so this time I interceded to diffuse the situation.

"Okay," I said, "let's all calm down, and we'll move on to the next person's presentation." I then turned back to Colleen. "Colleen, would you mind visiting with me after class? I would like to have you share your concerns about the presentation with me."

Thankfully, Colleen didn't argue further. She just nodded and then sat quietly looking at the floor the whole hour. When the class ended, she grudgingly followed me to my office. Once there, she again angrily denounced me, the class, and everything related to it. Her unhindered rant continued for quite a while.

When she finally stopped, I simply asked, "So what has happened?"

Colleen suddenly broke down and sobbed uncontrollably. After some time, her sobs subsided, and she told me her story.

"I married, and we moved clear across the country for my husband to go to school," she said. "We have two children. I have worked, supporting my husband and my family while he finished his degree and continued on through his doctorate. One day he came home and said he wanted a divorce. I thought it was just pressure from school, and I assured him we could get through it. But he said no. Eventually, I took the children and came here to go to school, trying to make a life for us while my husband and I finalized the divorce. I still believed we would eventually work things out, but this past weekend I flew out to meet with him and the divorce lawyers and . . ."

She started to sob again, and it took a while before she could speak. Eventually, she continued. "I found out the reason for the divorce had nothing to do with pressure from school, but that he has been having affairs with all of the young underclassmen girls the whole time we have been married."

I just listened while she talked. When she finished, she wiped away her tears. "Professor Howard, I don't really hate you, or the class, or even the project. I just hate life right now, and I don't know if I can make it."

I patted her arm. "I think you're stronger than you know. You'll get through this."

She attempted to smile. "I appreciate your confidence. I need it right now."

"Don't worry about the presentation until you feel you're ready," I said.

Throughout the rest of the semester, Colleen stopped by quite often just to visit. I did very little besides listen, but I did watch her as she worked through the divorce and grew stronger. As she created a new life, her confidence in herself flourished.

When the day came that she felt she could do her presentation, she gave a powerful delivery from the depths of her experiences.

As for me, I was grateful I had learned to have a little understanding.

An Evil Genius

✦

I had watched my student, Colleen, grow strong as she worked through her divorce and started a new life for herself and her two children. So I was surprised the next semester when she came into my office crying. She flopped into a chair and spoke through her tears.

"Professor Howard, I have to drop out of school."

"Why?" I asked in surprise.

"I don't have the money to continue. My ex-husband's lawyer got the judge to agree that if I took the children out of state, I had to pay for my ex's airline tickets to come see them. I appealed to the judge, telling about my husband's infidelity, but he didn't seem to care. And if my ex keeps demanding more visits, I won't be able to afford tuition."

"Does he have a reason he wants to see the children?" I asked.

"No. In fact, the last time I flew him up here, he didn't even come see the children. He went hunting with his buddies."

"That's not fair," I replied.

"What's not fair is that while he was in graduate school having affairs with all the young undergraduate girls, he was hiding away money that I earned, planning all along to pay for a divorce lawyer. Then when he demanded a divorce, I could hardly afford a lawyer at all. And now he and his little floozy wife just . . ."

I interrupted her. "Wait a minute. He's married already?"

Colleen nodded. "He's married to a girl who is probably still in her late teens, about ten years younger than he is. He married her about a week after the divorce was finalized."

"Colleen," I said slowly, "I think you're appealing to the wrong judge."

"What do you mean?" she asked.

"I think it's time you wrote a letter to his wife and thanked her for being willing to let her husband come visit you."

"But he doesn't visit us. He just goes off with his buddies to . . ."

I raised my eyebrows and Colleen paused, trying to understand what I was saying.

"You see," I said, "with his reputation of cheating and lying, what happened when he came up here doesn't matter as much as what his wife thinks happened. If he would cheat on you with her, why wouldn't he cheat on her with you?"

Colleen grinned. "So you mean, let her think that he has ulterior motives for coming up here?"

"Maybe it is a little underhanded, but what he is doing is unfair. You won't have to lie. With his reputation, even a simple thank-you will cause her to question his excursions."

Colleen laughed. "Professor Howard, that is almost evil. But I love it! I'm going home to write the letter right now."

She left and was back in less than a week. She bounced into my office and pulled up a chair.

"The thank-you letter worked like a charm!" she said. "I'm sure my ex's wife had barely received it before he called me. Apparently, when he arrived home, she demanded to know what he had been doing while he was visiting us. He told her he didn't visit us. That was the truth, but she didn't buy it for a minute. The more he tried to convince her of that fact, the less she believed him. She told him if he came to visit me again, she had to come along.

"He called, insisting I buy his wife a ticket, too. I told him to take a hike. He talked to his lawyer, and his lawyer told him no judge would make me do that, and if he wanted to take his wife, he would have to pay her airfare. My ex said he was not about to do that, partly because of the money and partly because he didn't want her to come anyway. That really made his wife suspicious. So he called me again, wanting me to tell his wife he hadn't visited us. I told him I wouldn't get involved."

"The sad thing is," I said, "he has lied so much that now, when he is telling the truth, his wife can't trust him."

Colleen grinned. "What matters is that they have canceled all of his trips up here, which means I can afford to stay in school." She handed me a plate of cookies. "These are for you. You are a genius." Her grin widened. "An evil genius, but a genius."

I smiled. I never thought I would consider being called an evil genius a compliment.

Halloween-type Traditions

Throughout our travels through Peru, our university group spent many hours studying old churches, archeological digs, and ancient artifacts. As much as I enjoy such historical landmarks, what I loved most was to see how common people lived. I was especially intrigued by our visit to Ollantaytambo in the sacred valley of the Inca, where I learned some very interesting traditions.

In Ollantaytambo, while most of our party milled around in the streets exploring the shops, I visited homes, that were designated on our tour brochures as being safe for foreigners. At each of these homes there was someone sitting outside the door, hoping for money from tourists. In English, with a mixture of what little Spanish I knew, I would ask if I could see inside. They would always answer in broken English, "One sol or one dolla'."

A person could get three sol (Peruvian money) to a dollar, so it was cheaper to use that. For that reason, we always joked that we didn't want to lose our sol while we were in Peru.

In the first home I entered, as the owner showed me around, I immediately noticed guinea pigs running everywhere. The owner pointed at them, then signaled to his mouth, indicating that they were food. I had learned that guinea pigs were a delicacy there. The guinea pigs ran in and out of the house and courtyard as freely as the chickens did.

Something in that particular home quickly caught my attention. There were three recesses in the wall, each a type of small cathedral-shaped alcove a couple of feet deep. In front of each was a stone altar. The alcoves were filled with small, white skulls about the size of the ceramic ones sold in the United States for Halloween decorations.

When I asked him if they were decorations, he seemed quite

offended. Though we struggled to communicate, I soon learned that these were skulls of his ancestors, which he had brought home so he could honor them. In turn, he said his ancestors watched over and protected him and his family. The things on the altars were offerings to them.

That first home I entered, which had about fifty skulls, was probably the oldest I visited. As I visited other homes in the valley, I found that most of them only had a few skulls, almost none of which had been shrunk like those in the first house. But every home I entered had at least two and followed the same tradition.

The owner of one home spoke a fair amount of English and was able to explain more about their ancestral traditions.

"We have day like what you call Halloween. We call Day of Dead."

"What do you do on the Day of the Dead?" I asked.

"We celebrate happiness of ancestors. We go to cemetery. We take picnic. Sometimes we have fire—roast guinea pig. We sing many songs and have happy time with ancestors."

"Do you think they come to visit you?" I asked.

He nodded. "We think they come, sing with us, and eat food." He paused momentarily, then said, "So me hear of Halloween in United States. What you do?"

"Well," I said, beginning to wonder how it would sound. "We dress up in costumes."

"What costumes?"

"All sorts," I replied. "Ghosts, goblins, witches, princesses, kings. Pretty much anything."

"Why you do this?" he asked.

I shrugged. "I'm not really sure. I guess mostly for fun and tradition. But once the children are dressed up, they go around to different houses, and people give them candy."

He wrinkled his brow and said, "Me think you have strange traditions."

I smiled because that is exactly what I was thinking about his.

A Lesson Learned

My daughter Heather came home from grade school almost in tears. She had worked hard on a school project, but when the graded papers were passed back, there wasn't one for her. She had seen the one she knew was hers in the possession of a boy who sat near her. She could tell he had erased her name and had written his in its place.

This boy would often lean over, trying to copy her work. She always tried to protect it from him, but he was quite persistent. Now, when she saw him claiming credit for her work, she could hardly contain her emotions.

When she talked to the teacher about it, the teacher was sympathetic but didn't know what evidence there was to prove it. She said all she could do was to allow Heather to redo the paper. That was why Heather was understandably upset when she came home.

"I worked so hard on that paper. It's just not fair. I shouldn't have to redo it."

I felt for her. I knew she truly had worked hard on it, but I could see no other option.

"Redo it and do an even better job the second time," I replied. "And Heather, unless you want him to do that again, make sure you put your name on your papers in pen."

"I will," she said. "But I wish there was a way to teach him a lesson."

"Well, there is one thing you might do," I replied.

"What's that?"

"Once, when I had someone copying my papers, I made sure the work they saw was not my best work. They soon learned it wasn't worth it to cheat off of me."

Heather hatched some plans of her own that almost made redoing the assignment bearable. In addition, she fixed things she realized she had done wrong the first time through the project. Her second paper was almost perfect, receiving an A. She later found out that her first paper, which the boy had taken, had only received a B. That made her feel somewhat avenged.

She also put her first plan into effect. The next time the students were working on an assignment in class, she knew the boy was copying her paper, so she made sure that every answer she wrote down was wrong. Then, during lunch hour, she redid all of it, putting the correct answers down before they turned the papers in. When the boy received his graded paper back with a zero on it, he seemed stunned. But he was even more so when he found out Heather received an A on hers.

He began to realize something was up, but that still didn't stop the cheating. So Heather decided to do something more. On the next paper she completed, she again made sure all of her answers were wrong. When it was time to turn the paper in, she put her name on it in pencil and passed it up the row. She watched as the boy slyly slipped her paper out of the stack and started to erase her name.

While he was busy doing that, she handed in another paper with the right answers. She passed it across to another row so he wouldn't see it. On that one she had written her name in pen. The boy didn't notice her second paper and turned in her first one with his name replacing hers.

On the day they received their papers back, the boy seemed shocked—first to see that Heather received a paper, and second, to find that the one with his name had received a zero.

It would be nice to say that he didn't copy Heather's work again, but that would be false. But he had learned a lesson.

A Doggone Cold Night

$+$

My assistant scoutmaster, Jubal, and I were taking the boys on a winter campout. We tried to go every month no matter the weather. We camped even in extreme cold, trying to teach the boys survival in the most severe conditions.

On this particular winter campout, we were going out on the desert north of where we live. There is hardly any place colder. The arctic air flows across it like an icy river penetrating clear through a person until the marrow freezes in the core of his bones.

When Jubal showed up at the church where we were meeting, his dog Cheyenne was riding in the back of his pickup. He saw me glance at her questioningly. He shrugged. "I tried to get her to stay home, but she insisted on coming with us."

I knew Cheyenne well. She had come along on many campouts. She loved the boys, and they loved her. But mostly she just loved the campfire and going somewhere new. However, I was concerned for her.

"It's really cold," I said. "Aren't you afraid she's going to be miserable?"

Jubal nodded. "I wanted her to stay home so she could sleep in the barn, but the minute she saw me throw my sleeping bag into my truck, she knew where I was going. She jumped in and refused to get out."

We decided there was nothing we could do about it. We needed to get to our campsite and settle in for the night, so we headed on our way. There was only the slightest bit of light left by the time we started pitching our tents, and I started up the fire for our dinner.

We all shivered around the fire, eating fajitas and telling stories. When it came time for bed, I heated some water, and we finished the evening with hot chocolate.

I had brought lots of extra blankets to make sure the boys were warm. I had planned on saving some for myself, but the temperature continued to drop. As we settled in for the night, the thermometer reported a solid twenty degrees below zero. To make sure the boys were warm enough, I ended up giving them all but one of my blankets. Jubal's sleeping bag was thick and warm, but mine wasn't. Without the extra blankets, I knew it was going to be a long, cold night.

As we climbed into our tent, Cheyenne whined to come in, but our tent was only a three-man tent, not built for two men and a dog. I long ago realized that whoever rates tents must measure them against people who are under five feet tall and as thin as pipes. With our two sleeping bags, there was no extra room. Cheyenne seemed to understand and lay down outside.

In the middle of the night, I was awakened by a noise. Suddenly sharply aware of my almost insensibly frozen feet, I began to shiver uncontrollably in the cold. I heard the noise again and looked to see Cheyenne pushing the tent zipper up with her nose.

I felt sorry for her, and I reached over and pulled up the zipper. Cheyenne slipped in, shivering, and I zipped the tent closed. Though I wasn't sure about having her in the tent with us, she was good and lay down at my feet. I lay there shivering for quite a while when suddenly I realized my feet, which were tucked underneath her, were starting to get warm. I reached down and patted her head, and she scooted up beside me.

The next morning when Jubal awoke and saw Cheyenne asleep beside me on my sleeping bag, he started to apologize.

"Don't worry about it," I said. "I was freezing and so was she. Together we warmed each other up."

"You're not upset?" he asked.

I laughed. "As far as I'm concerned, if we ever camp on a night this cold again, Cheyenne is welcome to sleep on my sleeping bag."

A Thanksgiving Concert

†

It was the evening before Thanksgiving, and David stood in the stage wing ready to make his entrance. It was to be his debut performance at one of the biggest, most famous concert halls in the world.

As the announcer welcomed the crowd and talked about the many things they had to be grateful for, David considered his own list. At the very top was his father. David smiled as he thought about him. His father was a strong man with big, rough, weathered hands from years of hard farm work. To provide for his family, he had constantly labored in both the heat of the summer sun and in the freezing cold of winter.

David had often been reminded that his father had been one of the greatest athletes the state had ever known. The trophy case at the high school back home was full of football, wrestling, and track trophies David's father had won or had helped win. It seemed as if everyone expected David to follow in the footsteps of his father and become a great athlete, too.

But in his very first fifth-grade wrestling match, David had done horribly. He was pinned in under a minute. When he came off the mat to face his father, David hung his head.

His father knelt down in front of him and said, "David, your heart wasn't in it."

David started making excuses, but his father stopped him. "David, you don't have to pretend to be something you aren't. What do you want to do?"

David couldn't look his father in the eye as he spoke quietly. "I want to play the piano."

"Then why are you wrestling?"

David looked up in surprise. "I thought you wanted me to."

David's father spoke firmly. "Son, I have taught you to be honest, work hard, do good things, and be kind. Never once have I expected you to live your life as I have lived mine. As long as you live true to the values I have taught you, you live the life you want to live. I believe God has given you your own talents. It would be wrong for me to determine the path He has for you. That is between you and Him."

"Really?" David asked in surprise.

"Really. But there is one other thing I do expect."

"What?" David asked.

"I expect you to be the best at whatever you decide to be."

David smiled, hugged his father, and promised he would be. He immediately dropped the wrestling team and started practicing the piano, and his father spent hard-earned money to ensure David received lessons. Although his father knew little about music, he always hauled the whole family to each of David's recitals. People soon learned that as long as his father was around, it wasn't a good idea to make fun of David for what he had chosen to do.

When David played his first big concert, his father was there. When it ended, and the audience rose to their feet cheering, David's father was the first and the loudest. Once everyone else had left the hall, David's father wrapped him in a hug in his big, strong arms.

"I'm proud of you, son," he said. "I'm sure music like that will have its place in heaven. I just hope God has a place for an old, hard-working farmer."

David's thoughts returned to the present as the announcer spoke his name. As he stepped onto the stage, welcomed by a cheering crowd, he was overwhelmed with gratitude for a father who loved him enough to encourage him to be what he wanted to be.

And although he missed having his father there to cheer for him, he knew that somewhere in heaven God had found a special place for an old, hard-working farmer.

A Smelly Situation

✦

One thing I love about working at the university is the young people I have the opportunity to associate with. We recently had two young ladies spend a lot of time in our home. One of them, Laura, was in my math class. The other, Kathy, was one of my wife's Elementary Music Methods students. They happened to be roommates and were both city girls, unaccustomed to country life. I liked to take advantage of their naivety and tease them.

One night they came for dinner and stayed late, visiting and playing games with my daughters. It was after dark by the time they were left.

I cautioned them, "Drive carefully. This time of year there's a lot of animals on the road out here in the country."

They laughed. "We're used to cats and dogs crossing the road," Kathy said.

"I'm not talking about cats and dogs," I replied. "I'm talking about moose and skunks, deer and raccoons."

They smiled, and I could tell by the look on their faces that they didn't believe me.

"Moose and skunks?" they asked sarcastically.

"Here is something to remember," I told them. "If you come across both a moose and a skunk at the same time, avoid the moose and hit the skunk. The skunk will only make your car smelly, but hitting a moose is deadly."

"Are you serious?" Kathy asked. "A moose and a skunk together?"

"You never know," I replied. "I've heard that moose and skunks sometimes run together in herds to protect each other."

I watched them look at each other and roll their eyes. They obviously didn't believe me. The next day, as I was driving my children to school, we came across a huge, dead skunk in the middle of the road. We could smell it for nearly a mile before we saw it and continued smelling it for many miles after we had passed by. Obviously, someone had hit it only the night before. As I recalled my conversation with the two girls, I laughed and said to my daughters, "Laura and Kathy must have come across a moose and a skunk last night."

I, of course, was joking, because the odds of them being the ones that hit it was very small, and the probability of a moose and a skunk being together was almost zero. But later that day I received an interesting call from Laura.

"Hi, Professor Howard," she said. "Can I possibly park my car at your house for a few days?"

"Why?" I asked.

"Do you remember how you told us to be careful as we were driving home last night because we might see moose and skunks?"

"Yes," I replied.

"Well, we thought you were joking. But when we were on our way home, we suddenly saw a skunk up ahead, so I swerved into the other lane to avoid hitting it."

"That was smart," I answered.

"But just then a moose ran into the road in front of us, and I remembered what you told us about avoiding hitting the moose at all costs, even if it meant running over the skunk. So I swerved back into my lane to miss the moose like you said I should, and I hit the skunk dead on."

"With the emphasis on dead?" I asked.

"Yes," she replied. "And my car smells so bad that our apartment manager asked if I could find another place to park it until the smell goes away."

Even though I had indeed only been teasing, I was suddenly grateful I had mentioned what I had. If they had hit the moose, the collision probably would have killed them.

"I've learned my lesson," Laura continued. "And I have warned everyone I know to be careful driving because moose and skunks run together in herds."

Clean, Shiny Dishes

＋

My roommate, John, had grown up in a home of privilege with maids and cooks, never having to take care of himself. But just before he came to college, his family fell on hard times. That was how he ended up in the cheapest college housing available as one of my roommates.

The other eight of us came from less-than-affluent families and were used to the daily chores that came with taking care of ourselves. None of us had ever met before moving in, so for our first apartment meeting, we got to know each other and established a chore schedule for washing dishes, sweeping, mopping, etc.

We calculated that the sixteen weeks of the semester divided equally among the nine of us came out to around twelve days per person for each assignment. We voted to take each of these in two six-day rotations. I volunteered to take the first six days washing dishes, knowing that it was the toughest job, and that, as the semester progressed, life would become much busier. John chose the last of the rotations.

As we approached mid-semester, John's first turn was drawing near when he informed us that he had never washed dishes before and didn't know how to go about it.

"I'd be happy to teach you," I said.

He shook his head. "I've decided that I'll just hire a girl I know to wash them."

"No way!" Bryce protested. "We often need dishes washed early in the morning when some of us are still in bed. No girl is coming in here then."

Others gathered around, and everyone voiced their opposition to having a young lady in the apartment to do the dishes.

"First off," Jim said, "our apartment isn't nice enough to have a girl traipsing around it, and second off, some of the guys here don't dress modestly when they sleep."

"Besides," Steve added, "you should learn to do it to take care of yourself."

The consensus was definitely that John needed to do the dishes himself, and John finally conceded that he probably didn't have the money to hire someone anyway.

"Do you want me to help you the first time?" I asked.

"No," John replied. "That would feel weird. Just explain it all to me."

I took him to the kitchen and talked through it. "You wash the dishes in the right sink, filled about half full of warm water. Make sure you put in two squirts of soap from the bottle under the sink and stir it up. Rinse the dishes in the left sink and put them in the drying rack."

He smiled and nodded. "That doesn't sound too hard."

On John's first day of doing the dishes, Jim and Steve had made a nice dinner and invited the girls they were dating to join them.

"What is this chewy gray stuff in the stew?" Jim's date asked after a few bites.

Jim and Steve looked at each other. "We didn't put in any chewy gray stuff," Jim said.

Bryce laughed. "That's probably just burnt offerings from Jim and Steve's cooking."

But when Bryce sat down to eat his own dinner, he had chewy gray stuff, too. When I sat down to eat, I did as well. It finally dawned on us that it had to be on the dishes.

"John, did you wash these dishes?" Bryce asked him.

"Yes," John replied.

"And did you use soap like I told you?" I asked.

"Of course," John replied. "I used the soap in the big blue bottle under the sink. I took the lid off, turned it upside down, and squeezed it hard twice."

"We don't have any blue bottle of soap," Jim said. He looked underneath the sink and gasped. The new half-gallon bottle of floor wax that we had purchased was mostly empty.

"Yes, sir," I said, as the two girls rushed to spit their food in the trash. "There's nothing like floor wax to give your dishes that added shine while simultaneously giving your food that chewy texture that keeps you from coming back for more."

A Miracle in Disguise

✦

Andrew lay in the hospital bed trying to remember what had happened. Gradually it started to come back to him. His unit had come under heavy German bombardment as they fought their way east of Paris. Everyone had rushed for cover. The American forces had responded with a bombardment of their own.

The Germans had started to fall back but were still putting up stiff resistance. Then Andrew remembered hearing the whistling of incoming shells. He had thrown himself to the ground, and after that he could remember no more.

As he looked around, Andrew could tell he was in an army hospital. Suddenly he became aware of a tremendous pain in his right arm. He winced and glanced toward it. The sight hurled him into a sudden and intense shock; where his arm was supposed to be, the sheet lay limp against the bed.

As he lay there gasping at the shock, someone spoke to him.

"It's about time you awoke. How are you feeling?"

Andrew could only exclaim between gasps, "My arm!"

The doctor nodded. "There was nothing much we could do. There was basically nothing left of it when you arrived. It was all we could do to save your life."

Another voice, a woman's, joined the doctor's. "You are fortunate, young man. Doctor Jacobson is the best. If you had ended up at a different medical unit, you likely wouldn't be alive."

"Thanks for the compliment, Mary," Doctor Jacobson said, "but there are many capable doctors."

Andrew, still suffering from the shock of losing his arm, wished to be left alone, and Doctor Jacobson seemed to understand. He excused himself, and the nurse followed his cue.

Andrew lay there alone, lost in his thoughts. Back in Kansas, before he was drafted, his life had revolved around music. He had won many piano competitions and had planned to make that his career. Now that dream was gone.

Andrew's father had been so proud of his son's piano ability. Having lost his left arm during World War I, Andrew's father said he enjoyed watching Andrew do something he himself couldn't do.

Andrew had watched his father struggle to do the simple things others took for granted. But his father never complained and worked hard to provide for his family.

After a while, Doctor Jacobson returned. "How are you feeling?" he asked.

"Okay," Andrew said.

"I have the strangest déja vu feeling when I look at you," Doctor Jacobson said.

"Why's that?" Andrew asked.

"Many years ago I fought in World War I. I was wounded and lay dying when my good friend came to my rescue. He saved my life but was wounded himself in the process. It was because of him that I decided to become a doctor. The crazy thing is, you look just like him, and he lost his arm, too."

Andrew felt a strange feeling come over him. "What was his name?" he asked.

"John Fredrickson," the doctor answered.

Andrew gasped at hearing his father's name. "Where was he from?"

"Kansas," Doctor Jacobson said.

The doctor who saved Andrew's life had himself been saved by Andrew's father. That was when Andrew remembered something his father always said: "A coincidence is nothing but a miracle in disguise."

A New Understanding

✦

Andrew had been wounded and consequently lost his right arm fighting in World War II. He had planned to make a career as a professional musician, but that dream was gone. In the hospital, Andrew was surprised to learn that the doctor who saved his life had himself been saved by Andrew's father in World War I. And the surprises didn't end there.

"Did your father ever tell you how he and I became friends?" Doctor Jacobson asked.

Andrew shook his head. "He didn't talk about the war much."

"We met one night when the troops gathered for entertainment. Everyone was disappointed to learn that the entertainers were sick. Our commander knew that John, your father, played the piano because he had played previously for the officers. So he told John to play. I considered myself a singer, so I volunteered to join him. We were a hit."

"Wait a minute," Andrew interjected. "My father played the piano?"

"Yes," Doctor Jacobson answered. "He was incredibly good. He said he hoped someday to make himself a career in musical entertainment."

"He never mentioned that."

"I'm sure I know why," Doctor Jacobson replied. "We performed our way across much of Europe as our unit moved closer and closer to the front. And then came the day we arrived at the fighting. There was no piano, and there was certainly no time for entertainment. We were ordered to move forward, but we instantly fell under heavy bombardment.

"Our unit was forced to fall back, but I was hit by shrapnel and fell wounded in the no man's land between the two armies. I could feel the life draining out of me, and I was sure I was going to die. I can still remember, as the daylight faded, seeing the shadow of a man crawling toward me. It was your father.

"Under fire, he was hit by bullets that ripped his left arm apart, but he still wouldn't leave me. With his one good arm, he pulled me back to our line. I lost my leg, and he lost his arm.

"He was saddened by the loss of his arm, and although he tried once more to play the piano with one hand, he quit, saying he would never attempt to play again. He said that with his left arm gone there could be no harmony in his music and no harmony in his life."

Suddenly, Andrew understood more about his father than he ever had before. His father had always been proud when Andrew won piano competitions and received the accolades of adoring audiences. Andrew hadn't realized that his father had once been in his same shoes but had lost that opportunity defending his country.

And yet Andrew's father had never complained nor indicated any kind of jealousy. Instead, he had supported Andrew and had done everything he could to help him excel. Andrew's father had even worked a second job to make sure Andrew received the very best piano lessons. And best of all, his father was always the first on his feet cheering when Andrew performed a concert.

Andrew wondered if his father somehow found joy in his son's accomplishments because piano performance had been his own dream. But how would he feel now? Would he feel the same disappointment at the loss of Andrew's arm as he had at the loss of his own?

Andrew was in the hospital for a couple of months, during which time he never wrote home about the loss of his arm. When he learned that he was to be released and would be returning home in time for Christmas, he had mixed feelings.

As Andrew was preparing to leave, Doctor Jacobson handed him a wrapped package. "This is a present for you and your father. Don't open it until you can open it together on Christmas."

Doctor Jacobson then bid Andrew farewell, reminding him of the lesson they had both learned from Andrew's father. "Remember that a coincidence is nothing but a miracle in disguise."

Harmony and Melody

✦

Andrew lost his right arm fighting in World War II. He had planned to make a career playing music, but that dream was now gone. Having never known that his father played the piano at all, Andrew was surprised to learn that his father had also dreamed of making a career in music until he had lost his own arm fighting in World War I. Andrew wondered if that was why he had been so proud of Andrew's musical accomplishments.

During his many months in the army hospital, Andrew never wrote in any of his letters home about the loss of his arm. Now it was Christmas, and he was heading home, but all he could think about was his father. What would he think now that Andrew could no longer play the piano?

Andrew's whole family was at the train station to welcome him home. He knew they could not help but notice that his arm was missing, but no one said anything. They hugged him and gave him a hero's welcome, but still doubt lingered in his mind about what others truly thought of him—especially his father.

When he walked into their home and saw the old piano, the nice one that his father had worked a second job to buy for him, he could not face his feelings any longer and turned and walked out the door. But in the stillness of the evening air, he could hear the crunch of snow behind him and turned to find his father following him.

Andrew turned from his father and spoke quietly. "Not much of a Christmas present, is it? I guess I'll never be the great musician you dreamed I would be."

Andrew's father wrapped his arm around Andrew's shoulders. "It's the best Christmas present in the world to have my son, of whom I am very proud, come home. You may not be able to do the things you once dreamed of, but it is the goodness of your heart that brings me the greatest happiness."

"Why did you never tell me you used to play the piano?" Andrew asked.

Andrew's father was quiet for a moment before he spoke. "Where did you hear that?"

"The doctor who saved my life said that you and he used to perform together and that you lost your arm saving him during a battle. Why didn't you ever tell me?"

Andrew's father turned from him and spoke quietly. "I guess I never felt like I was good enough. I tried to play once, but without the harmony of my left hand, I felt less than adequate. I guess that is how I have felt all of my life—less than adequate in everything."

"No, Father, you're wrong!" Andrew exclaimed. "In the thing that matters most—being a father—you are the greatest there is! You have done things with one hand that many men couldn't do with two. And if my heart is great, it is because yours is greater."

Andrew could see the tears roll down his father's face. He reached out and hugged him, then pulled back and said, "Oh, there's one more thing. Doctor Jacobson sent a present for both of us."

They returned to the house to open the package together. Inside they found some music with a handwritten letter. The top few music pages were crossed out. The note said, "Dear John, Years ago when you said you would never play the piano again because you had lost the harmony from your life, I set about to write a song for you that could be played by one hand. The top pages were my attempts, and though I feel they were good, it seems there are greater possibilities for you. When I met your son, I began to realize two things. First, as you always said, a coincidence is nothing but a miracle in disguise, and second, sometimes in life we can, ourselves, play both melody and harmony, but sometimes it requires more than one to make the music complete. This song is for both you and your son. Your friend, Private (Doctor) Jacobson."

They removed the crossed-out pages and found a song entitled "Harmony and Melody." Andrew looked at his father who smiled and nodded. They sat down at the piano, Andrew on the left and his father on the right, and they played, combining their abilities to make the whole. At first, they made a lot of mistakes and the music was rough, but it wasn't long before it sounded like one person was performing.

And every Christmas after that, until Andrew's father passed away, father and son played "Harmony and Melody" together. After Andrew's father's death, Andrew played his part alone.

Each time he ended, he always said, "Dad, I hope you're still practicing, so when I join you we can make harmony and melody complete—again."

A Final Chorus

✦

Bill Farley, a good friend of our family, has been a great support over the years. When I wrote my first musical, Bill cheered us on and encouraged us. His daughter, Jennifer, played in the orchestra for the performance of my musical. Another daughter, Jaime, was one of my daughter's best friends.

Bill was always good for an uplift and a smile. He turned forty about the same time I did, followed by both of our wives a couple of years later. One time when we got together, he was teasing his wife about this new decade of her life.

"I'm not sure what I think about being married to someone who is forty," he teased her. "It makes me feel strange knowing I'm married to someone who could be a grandma. Maybe I should trade you in for two twenty-year-olds."

His sharp-witted wife said, "Bill, you aren't wired for 220."

Bill enjoyed his job at the local high school teaching both band and choir, and the young people loved him. His sense of humor and relaxed style helped the students feel calm and enjoy the music, even when performing concerts.

Bill laughed as he talked about his choir concerts and his love for the students. "Whenever I have a concert, we always end with the 'Hallelujah Chorus.'"

Both my wife, Donna, and I were amazed at that. "That has got to be quite an undertaking with a high school choir," I said.

Bill just grinned. "Maybe. But really, it's just a gimmick. That way my students and I are always guaranteed a standing ovation."

I laughed. That was so typical of Bill.

But there was one thing for which I admired Bill more than anything else. Some years ago, Bill and his daughter Jaime were diagnosed with cancer at nearly the same time. We watched as the two of them fought it, supporting each other through chemotherapy, and facing together the many other trials that go along with cancer. There were times when everyone thought the cancer had been beaten only to have it return. Through it all, both Bill and Jaime were positive. Their cheerfulness always lifted those around them. They seldom showed any discouragement, and they were never bitter or resentful at the part life had given them to play.

Eventually, Jaime passed away. The trials she had faced, as trials often do, had made an angel out of her. Everyone loved and missed her, but I don't think anyone missed her more than Bill did.

Bill's cancer worsened again, and only a week or so after Jaime passed away, the prognosis for him turned dismal. The doctor informed Bill that he only had a few more weeks to live. As he grew weaker, his sweet wife tenderly cared for him, and Bill set a goal to live past Christmas so as not to put a damper on that special day.

When we visited with him, Bill was cheerful and upbeat. He talked of the students he loved and the music program he had spent his life building. But mostly, he talked about what joy it would be to see Jaime again. Anyone going to cheer him up at this tough time of his life found instead that they came away cheered.

Bill didn't make it past Christmas. Instead, it was on that very day that he went to join Jaime. Perhaps it was fitting that the very day the final song of his concerts celebrated was the day the concert of Bill's life ended.

And for those of us who were privileged enough to know him, we are positive of one thing: We would give him a standing ovation for the life he has lived, and he wouldn't even need to sing the "Hallelujah Chorus" to get it.

Deep Snow

✦

In the mountains, there are a lot of very expensive homes that wealthy people call their summer cabins. The snow up there will often reach ten feet or more in depth.

A friend of mine, David, has a job filling propane tanks around the valley. Quite often calls will come in from homeowners who are away for the winter to fill propane tanks. If the tanks go empty, the heat in the homes will shut off, and the water pipes will freeze and crack.

The problem is that the deep snow often conceals the tanks. Smart homeowners will set a tall flag so the tanks can be found. Some, however, do not, in which case David has to either rely on a map of the property call the homeowner and rely on the owner's memory.

If the map or the directions are not good, David might dig down the ten-foot depth only to find that the tank isn't there. He then expands the circle, digging wider and wider. Although the homeowner must pay extra for David's time, it can be tiring work.

One day, David came to fill our tank. He looked cold and exhausted.

"So, how has your day been?" I asked.

He sighed wearily. "I'm beat. At the first house I went to, the homeowner said he had a flag on his tank. When I arrived, I could see two small red flags, each sticking up about a foot above the snow."

"Did he have two tanks?" I asked.

"I thought he might," David replied, "but usually the tanks would be side by side with one flag between them. I didn't know what else to do, so I went to one of the flags and started digging. I dug down nearly ten feet, which took about an hour. Finally, I hit something solid, but it wasn't the tank. It was a four-wheeler someone had forgotten to park in the garage, and it had one of those tall flags that people put on them so they're visible over hills while they're riding.

"I was tired and unhappy, but I went to the other flag and started digging. I dug down to that one and found another stupid four-wheeler. I climbed out of that hole and looked around, and far off by the shop I saw another flag I hadn't seen previously. I dug down to it and hit a trampoline frame."

"I think I would have called the owner and told him to dig out his own tank," I said.

"I felt like it," David replied, "but he buys thousands of gallons each year, so my boss would have been mad. I called the homeowner three times. He couldn't remember where the tank was, so he guessed. Twice more I dug in the wrong place. Finally, the third time I called him, he suddenly remembered that he had put the trampoline frame over his tanks. The hole I had dug by the shed was where they were. I just had to go down further. I was so mad I could spit, but my spit probably would have just frozen in my mouth."

"I hope your other stops went better," I said.

David shook his head. "I only had time for one more before coming here. For that one I had a map. I estimated by the map, dug the first hole, and hit a picnic table. It took me three phone calls and three more tries to find the tanks."

"You're a lot more patient than I am," I said. "I obviously couldn't do what I would like because of the freezing pipes, but I know what I would feel like doing."

"What's that?" he asked.

"I think that after I dug the first hole, I'd want to just haul my propane hose in there, fill the picnic table, and be on my way."

Slime and Punishment

+

Little Harvey's family was going to visit some good friends who lived on a ranch. He excitedly put on his new white T-shirt. His large family didn't have a lot of money, and new shirts were hard to come by, so he was proud of it and wanted to enjoy it on this special occasion.

When they arrived at the ranch, Harvey's family followed their friends out to look at the animals. In one small pasture was a little herd of baby calves.

"These calves are a bit sick," the rancher said. "Don't you kids go chasing them."

"What kind of sickness do they have?" Harvey's father asked.

"Scours," came the reply.

Harvey didn't know what scours was. He also hadn't considered chasing the calves until the farmer mentioned it was taboo, but now the thought of running after one and catching it sounded fun. The group continued on to other things. Harvey followed them for a short distance, but the thought of chasing the calves soon drew him back to the small pasture. He envisioned himself a small cowboy, and he knew he just had to catch a calf.

Harvey soon discovered that the calves could run faster than he had ever imagined. Even though they weren't very old, he found it difficult to keep up with them. After chasing them for some time, he learned which one was the slowest and singled it out for his personal calf-capture competition.

The calf ran fast, but Harvey could see that he was gaining on it. He was just at the point where he could reach out and grab the calf's tail when its back end exploded like a liquid shotgun, drenching Harvey from head to toe in green and yellow slime. That was when

Harvey learned that scours was a form of diarrhea.

For just an instant, Harvey stood there in shock, somewhat suffocated from the smell. But after he wiped his face enough so that he could see, he remembered his T-shirt. He looked down and found that it was almost totally green and yellow. He rushed to the water trough and tried to wash it out, and although the stain faded somewhat, he knew it would never be completely white again.

Not knowing what else to do, he tossed his shirt into some weeds and hurried to catch up to the others, hoping no one would notice. But a shirtless boy is hard to miss.

"Harvey, where's your shirt?" his mother asked.

Harvey shrugged. "I don't know. I guess I must have lost it."

A person doesn't just lose a shirt, especially not a new one. Everyone spread out to search for it, and as people were getting close to the weeds where it was hidden, Harvey retrieved it and threw it into the calf pen. When the others came near enough to see him, he picked it up.

"I found it! Look what those stupid calves did to my shirt," he said, trying to pretend that it was all an accident.

But once they discovered that the back of the shirt was still mostly white while the front was mostly green and yellow, it didn't take a master sleuth to figure out what Harvey had been up to.

And that was the day Harvey learned the punishment for lying was even more severe than the punishment for chasing sick calves. That is, as long as you don't mind a green-and-yellow T-shirt.

Wrestling Challenge

✦

I tried to avoid my roommate's challenges. I'm not sure why John felt the great need to prove that he was better than I was. He was tall, blond, and handsome. Girls hung around him like flies around a dung pile, never giving me a second look.

I got up at five o'clock each weekday morning to run the five miles my coach expected, and then I went to the gym and lifted weights. On my way back to our apartment, I passed John as he trotted across campus to the fieldhouse. He would be dressed in adult footie pajamas with a bathrobe over them, his bathrobe flying behind him like a peacock with loose tail feathers. He acted like he didn't know me, and with the way he was dressed, I was glad.

But with his obsession to beat me at things, it wasn't a big surprise when he challenged me to a wrestling match.

"Oh, for heaven sakes, John!" Bryce, our roommate, said. "Daris is a varsity wrestler. What makes you think you can beat him?"

"I'm bigger than he is," John answered, "and I wrestled in junior high."

"You might be taller," Jim chimed in, "but Daris has more muscle in one finger than you have in your whole body."

That made John really mad. "Well, if he's scared, I can understand," he retorted.

I hadn't said anything to that point. I had hoped to avoid this because John had a big ego, and I knew if I beat him he would hold a grudge for a long time.

"I'm not scared, John," I said. "But I don't think this kind of competition is good for roommate relations."

"Just admit you're afraid you'll get beat," John replied. "It's understandable."

As much as I wanted to take his challenge, I thought it was better not to. However, our other seven roommates felt it was time John learned a lesson.

"You're not going to let him talk to you that way, are you?" Steve asked me.

Before I could even answer, Bryce jumped in again. "Of course Daris is going to take the challenge! I'll reserve the wrestling room."

"All right," I said. "I'll take the challenge, but only if there are no girls there."

Even as John committed to my terms, he laughed. "Afraid you'll be embarrassed, huh?"

After John headed off to class, Bryce asked, "Why did you insist on that?"

"John would never forgive me if he loses in front of female spectators," I replied.

The day for the challenge arrived. I met my other roommates in the wrestling room. When John arrived, he had dozens of girls with him.

I pulled him aside. "John, you promised no girls."

He smirked. "You said you weren't afraid, so I knew you wouldn't mind."

I didn't want to go through with it, but John started mocking me, so I decided to continue. Bryce refereed. Within ten seconds after the whistle blew to start the match, I had John locked up in a pin. But Bryce didn't want to let John off that easy, so he only gave me points. The whole first round went the same way. By the time it ended, I was ahead twenty to nothing.

"Let me have top position, and I'll show you something!" John fumed.

I agreed, and John took top position. But once again it was only seconds after Bryce blew the whistle that I had John on his back. Toward the end of the second round, with the score thirty-five to nothing, Bryce finally called a pin. John stormed from the room with his female entourage swooning after him.

He stomped around our apartment for days, refusing to speak to any of us. When he finally did, he got right in my face.

"I can outrun you!"

Jim laughed. "John, you know how in the fieldhouse you might pass me once during your whole run? Well, when I go early, Daris passes me almost every lap."

"I have an idea," Bryce chimed in. "Let's invite all of your girlfriends and show you."

But that's one challenge I never had to take, and I'm glad. I look stupid in footie pajamas.

The Key of Togetherness

✦

As we finished our scout meeting, I reminded the boys about our upcoming plans. "Don't forget that next week is our monthly service meeting. We will be helping old Widow Rosting clean out her shed, so come an hour early and dress in old work clothes."

"Not another service project," Gordy grumbled. "Last time it took us so long we didn't get to do anything fun."

"This job might be interesting," I replied. "Have you ever gone through an old shed? You never know what strange things you might find."

That hardly ignited fires of excitement in them, but most of the boys still came. When we arrived at Widow Rosting's, she smiled.

"Thank you for doing this. I can't tell you what's in there. In addition to being an avid collector, my husband worked a lot of different jobs in his lifetime. If you find anything you would like, you're welcome to keep it."

That seemed to intrigue the boys, who chattered excitedly as I led the way to the shed. I lifted the hook that latched the door, and the door unwillingly squeaked open as I pushed against it. I stepped in, trying to find a light switch, and was engulfed in spider webs. I wrapped up the webbing and pulled it from my face and hair while I continued my search. I eventually found what I was looking for and clicked the switch, dimly lighting the shed with more shadows than light.

Some of the boys held back, reluctant to enter the dusty shed. Others rushed ahead of me, hoping to be the first to find something interesting. Soon the boys were scurrying all over. When a boy found a treasure, he would slip it into my van to take home with him. Junk was put into the pickup that belonged to my assistant, Rod.

I took a load of trash out, tossed it into Rod's truck, and turned around to find Gordy and Mort side by side, grinning at me.

"Guess what we found?" Mort said.

"A mummy?" I replied.

They laughed and then Gordy said, "Not quite. But something almost as good. Look at this."

They each held up a wrist, and between them was a pair of handcuffs. "Aren't they cool?" Mort asked.

I stared at them as they continued to grin and asked, "You do have a key, don't you?"

Suddenly, their grins disappeared as their predicament dawned on them.

Gordy turned to Mort. "You do have a key, right?"

"Me?" Mort replied. "It was your idea to put them on."

The other boys and Rod gathered around.

"Well, well," Rod said, looking at Gordy and Mort. "Don't you two make the cutest couple holding hands like that?"

"We aren't holding hands!" Gordy said. "Idiot Mort handcuffed us together."

"If I were to allow someone to handcuff themselves to me, they would have to be a lot better-looking than either of you two are," Rod said.

I laughed. "What I want to know is which of your houses you two plan to live at."

"Just shut up and find a key so I can get away from stupidilla before I'm infected with stupidness," Mort said.

"I think it might be too late for that," Devin smirked.

I told the boys to spread out and search for a key. We turned the shed upside down but still didn't find one. It grew time for the boys to go home, and we had hardly cleaned anything. We decided I should take the other boys home and notify Mort's and Gordy's parents while Rod took the two boys to the sheriff's office to get them separated.

When I inquired later, I learned that the only thing the sheriff's office had been able to do was cut the chain connecting the handcuffs.

Eventually, Rod took the boys to the fire department where they used equipment for cutting into cars to remove the handcuffs.

"I hope they've learned their lesson," I said.

Rod laughed. "Not likely. They're scouts."

Scout Logic

I was sure that since two of my scouts had handcuffed themselves together the week before and had to be taken to the fire department to get them apart, they had learned a lesson and would be more careful. We had been working on our service project cleaning old Widow Rosting's shed but had gotten very little done besides hunting for the handcuff's key. My scouts had hoped to have a game night the next week and weren't too happy about going back to finish the job.

"Hey," I said. "It wasn't my fault that Gordy and Mort handcuffed themselves together."

"Cleaning the shed isn't so bad," Devin reminded the others. "There are lots of cool old things in there."

We went back to work on the shed, and the boys were soon finding interesting things and enjoying themselves.

"What's this?" Dallin asked, holding up a rusty tin box.

"I'm surprised at you," I replied. "Haven't you ever seen an electric fence charger before?"

"Is that what it is?" Dallin asked. "I haven't seen one this old before."

"It's almost an antique," Devin said. "I bet it doesn't work anymore."

"I suppose you could plug it in and find out," Rod, my assistant, said, flashing me a grin.

"Great idea," Gordy replied. "Let's find an outlet."

I sidled up near Rod and whispered, "You know this is going to end badly, don't you?"

He nodded. "Of course. That's why it should be fun."

The boys eventually found an outlet on the outside of the shed.

They plugged in the charger and looked at it. "Now what?" Mort asked.

"Touch it and see if it works," Rod said.

"How stupid do you think I am?" Mort asked.

"Do you really want us to answer that after you and Gordy handcuffed yourselves together last week?" Devin asked.

"I'm sure it was just rhetorical," I answered.

"I heard that if you touch a wet piece of grass to a charger, it will sparkle," Gordy suggested.

The boys hunted for a piece of grass. After they had one, Gordy spat on it and touched it to the positive node. Nothing happened. Feeling brave, Gordy touched the node. Still nothing. Then he held on to the positive node with one hand and held the charger with the other. Nothing. "Old piece of junk," he said.

"I told you it wouldn't work," Devin said.

I knew that all of the boys had seen electric fences before, but none of them were from families that ran a lot of cattle. They were mainly used to farming, growing potatoes and grain, so they likely didn't have experience with what made the electrical charge of the fence work.

Rod whispered to me, "You're familiar with these old fence chargers, aren't you?"

I nodded. "I've worked with lots of them."

"Do you think it still works?" Rod asked.

"I've felt the jolt of ones older than this," I replied. "So I'm sure it probably does. These older models weren't too sophisticated and didn't break down easily."

"Then why do you think it isn't working?" Rod asked.

"It's really quite simple," I replied. "They aren't getting shocked because they aren't completing a full circuit. There has to be something grounding the negative node. As long as no one touches it, no one connects a wire to it, or nothing else grounds it, they will be fine."

"Of course," Rod laughed. "I should have realized that. I'm surprised no one has touched it yet."

By this time, the boys had all gathered around and were in a tight bunch looking at the charger.

Suddenly, Mort said, "I wonder what this other knob is for." He reached out and touched it, and suddenly almost everyone in the group screamed as the nonlethal charge gave them all a good jolt.

Rod grinned. "Good job, guys. I guess you proved the charger still works after all."

There Are Ways

✦

The nurse sighed. "Please, Kara. Before you have your surgery, we need a urine sample."

Kara shook her head. "I don't want to go, and there's no way you can make me."

Kara was twelve, going on thirteen. She was right at that age when a young girl wants to start asserting her independence. In addition, there are certain matters of privacy that become important to a girl who is approaching her teen years.

"Kara," the nurse said, "We have to have a urine sample. I also need to put in your IV, and it will be really hard for you to use the bathroom after I get the IV in. We can't take it back out, so you'll have to take it into the bathroom with you."

Kara still refused, so the nurse went out to inform the doctor. He came back in with her.

"So, Kara," the doctor said, "I understand that you are refusing to give us a urine sample. We don't need much. Can't you just give a little?"

Kara shook her head. "I think urine samples are gross, and I'm not going to do one."

"I know they can be, as you say, gross, but we still need one," the doctor said.

"Well, I'm not going to," Kara said. "I don't need to use the bathroom, and you can't make me."

The doctor smiled. "Oh, I see. Well, I guess there's nothing we can do to get you to give us a sample?"

"Nothing," Kara said defiantly.

The doctor, still smiling, turned to the nurse. "Kara says there is nothing we can do, so I suggest that we go ahead and start the IV."

The nurse nodded, smiling herself. "Yes, sir."

Kara looked away and felt a small poke. Soon the needle was in, and the nurse connected the IV to it.

The doctor grinned and told the nurse, "Turn it up to her full capacity. We need to get her ready for this surgery." The nurse nodded and did as she was told. The doctor turned to leave, saying, "Let me know when attitudes change and make sure the facility is ready."

Kara wondered what he meant by that. She watched as the nurse went out and came in again with a basin that hooked into the toilet seat. Kara grinned, watching her. If they thought they were going to get her to use the bathroom, they were sadly mistaken. She had made sure she used the bathroom before leaving home. In addition, surgery orders said she couldn't drink anything after dinner the night before, so there was nothing they could do.

Kara smiled to herself. This was one battle she was definitely going to win.

The nurse kept slipping in to check on her. Each time she did, she asked Kara if she needed to use the bathroom yet. Kara just grinned and shook her head. But it wasn't long before she did need to go. She was still sure it couldn't get too strong since she hadn't had anything to drink. But, finally, she could hold it no longer. As she got up to go, the IV alarm beeped. The nurse immediately came.

"I need to use the bathroom," Kara said.

"I'll have to help you since the IV has to go with you," the nurse replied.

Kara balked at the lack of privacy, but there was little she could do. If she didn't go, she would wet herself. She went, and the urine sample was collected. Once informed, the doctor came in.

"You can turn the IV down to a slow flow now," he told the nurse.

Kara learned two important lessons that day: one, what an IV does, and two, that hospitals do have ways of collecting urine samples from unwilling patients.

Pine Nuts

Leann received a call from her friend Sarah. "Hey, Leann, do you like pine nuts?"

"Of course," Leann said. "Who doesn't?"

"Well, they are in season. Would you like to pick some up? You can have all you gather."

"I'd love to," Leann said. "When can I come?"

"Feel free to help yourself," Sarah replied. "They are getting really ripe and need to be collected before they go bad. You know that big tree in our back yard? Just go through the gate by the side of the house and help yourself, even if I'm not home."

After Leann had hung up the phone, she turned to her husband. "Shawn, would you like to go to gather pine nuts with me?"

He shrugged. "I like pine nuts, but I've never gathered them before. I've only bought them at the store all shelled in a bag. To be honest, I'm not even sure I'd know what I was looking for."

Leann laughed. "I haven't ever gathered them either, but how hard can it be? We'll just go to the big pine tree, look under it, and there they'll be."

Shawn agreed to go with her, so a couple of days later they made their way to Sarah's house. Leann knocked on the door, but there was no answer, so she led Shawn through the side gate into the backyard. The big pine tree dominated the landscape. Leann and Shawn went to it.

"It looks like there are light brown ones and darker brown ones," Shawn said. "What's the difference?"

Leann picked up a light brown one. It felt really hard. She then picked up the dark brown one, which was much softer. Though

Leann wasn't really sure, she thought that the answer seemed quite obvious.

"I'm sure the dark brown ones have already lost their shells," she replied.

"But I thought you had to crack them," Shawn said.

"Well, the shells must obviously come off by themselves in nature," Leann replied. "How else would a baby tree grow?"

Shawn nodded, agreeing that must be true, and they set about picking up all of the pine nuts they could find. They collected basketfuls, throwing the light and brown ones in together.

Leann could hardly believe a single tree, even one this big, could produce that so many nuts. And there were far more dark brown ones than light brown. The dark ones were the nuts Leann was most interested in because they wouldn't need cracking, and the thought of shelling nuts hour after hour didn't thrill her.

After they were finished, Shawn loaded the baskets into their van while Leann raked all around the tree, making it as nice as possible. She felt that if her friend shared the pine nuts with them, the least she and Shawn could do was leave it clean.

When Leann looked in their full van, the basketfuls of pine nuts made her mouth water. She just had to eat some. As Shawn eased their van down the road, she took her water bottle and, holding a handful of the dark ones out the window, she poured water on them to wash the dirt off. When she was sure they were nice and clean, she tossed the whole handful into her mouth.

Instantly she gagged, spat them out the window, and rinsed her mouth. "Don't eat the dark brown ones," she said to Shawn. "They are horrible. They must have gone bad after they lost their shells."

Later that day, Sarah called her. "Leann, thanks for cleaning up under the pine tree. It looks great. But you didn't have to pick up all of the bunny poop."

"What color is bunny poop?" Leann asked suspiciously.

"Dark brown, of course," Sarah laughed.

Leann decided she would ask Shawn to spread the dark brown "pine nuts" on the garden for fertilizer.

What Students Learned In Math Class 2016

＋

Over the years, I have found that one of the students' greatest criticisms of any math class is their claim that they didn't learn anything. Therefore, as part of their final, I have the students list ten things they have learned. These items can be anything at all in relation to the class. They are allowed to write their list ahead of time and bring it to the final if they want. Most observations are quite normal, but some make for interesting reading. Below are my favorites from this year.

1) I have learned not to take a junior/senior level math class my freshman year.

2) Wait until after the class review day to take the test.

3) People complain about having to walk up the hill to the math building even though most people really need the exercise. I'm not saying I need it, but some people really do.

4) Don't write in pen.

5) The boy that sits behind me is correct a lot less often than he thinks he is.

6) Study sessions should not be held in my apartment when my roommates are home.

7) Sitting in the front rows of class is a good idea. Probably not the front row, however, because there is too much chalk dust. But if a person gets too many rows back there are too many distractions to pay attention to the teacher.

8) I have found that I am much better at math if I schedule my math classes in the mornings when I am most alert. I can't stay awake for math in the afternoon.

9) In the probability section, I learned that the reason there are treads on shoes is to give the ants a 50-50 chance. Actually, I learned that it depends on how much tread there is. It's complicated.

10) I learned that it is ridiculous that we have to take foundations courses like this one when we already know the stuff. I already had stats in high school, so I didn't learn anything in the class other than loans, investment, logic, probability, and taxes.

11) I learned that I have little patience for wasting time in class and that I value my time and learning. However, I have found that if I miss one class, I am lost and totally tune myself out, so I need to have more patience there.

12) Penny bidding sites are fun until you lose all of your money on them.

13) I learned how to do taxes and why people are so willing to pay someone else to do them.

14) I had just learned that the cute girl next to me was named Hailey, and then she dropped the class.

15) I learned I will not let another one of my sisters plan her wedding for the middle of a semester and make me miss class for it.

16) I learned not to take Nyquil before taking a test. I sat down to take my test and the next thing I knew it was two hours later, the testing center was closing, and I hadn't even finished reading problem one.

17) I learned that I could survive in an apartment with five other girls for three months. But I was glad when it was over.

18) I learned that I take a lot of things for granite. *[I'm sure he meant granted.]*

19) I learned that adult life is harder than I thought.

20) I learned that some things are better left for the calculator to figure out.

21) When I text in class, I miss important information.

22) I learned that I actually need to study for exams.

23) I learned that two o'clock in the morning is not a good time to finish homework.

24) I learned how not to get punched by a girl when I am teasing her.

25) I learned that math and I are still enemies and that we'll never get along.

What to Look for in a Girl

✦

I was scoutmaster to eighteen boys. On Tuesday nights I handled the scouting activities, and on Sundays, another man taught them while I simply participated. But one week, after he finished the Sunday lesson and everyone was leaving, he stopped me.

"Daris, I would like you to teach the lesson next week."

"Are you going to be gone?" I asked.

He shook his head. "No, I just don't know how to approach the topic."

He handed me the manual, and when I arrived home, I opened it up and looked at the lesson. The title was "The Importance of a Good Marriage."

Instantly I realized his dilemma. That lesson might work for boys that were sixteen to eighteen, but not for boys who were twelve to fourteen. It wasn't that they didn't want to talk about girls; they just didn't know how to go about it. Conversations around the campfire of that nature were awkward. One boy might start by saying to another, "I think your sister is cute." At which point the second boy would say, "You must have a mental condition! Don't get near me. I don't want to catch it." And that would be the end of the conversation.

I spent a lot of time thinking about the lesson and had an idea.

When Sunday came, speaking to the loudest, most talkative boy, I said, "Gordy, I need you to write on the chalkboard for me." He happily took his position. I then turned to the other boys. "I want all of you to tell Gordy everything you want in the girl you plan to marry."

The look of shock on their faces wasn't unexpected, but eventually, Mort grinned and started it off. "She needs to be pretty."

"Yeah," Devin said. "And rich."

Soon the boys were throwing out ideas faster than Gordy could write, and he had to write faster and abbreviate. Within twenty minutes there were four columns with about fifteen things in each. When they had basically run out of ideas and board space, I started the next phase.

"Now," I said, "you have to narrow it to three."

"Three?" Dallin gasped. "That's crazy!"

"You better make sure you keep the three that are most important to you," I replied. "I may give suggestions, but I won't tell you what to choose."

"Well, I suppose that cooking good pies could come off," Mort said reluctantly.

Some of the boys argued briefly, but eventually Gordy erased it. Gradually the lists grew smaller.

When they debated taking off "pretty," I said, "Guys, you will sit across the table from her all of your life. I'm not saying she has to be drop-dead gorgeous, but she should be attractive to you." They decided to leave it.

When they debated about whether she should be rich, I again gave a suggestion.

"When you say she is rich, where did she get her money?" I asked.

"From her dad, of course," Mort replied.

"And do you think he's going to give his money to you?" The boys paused and looked at each other. I added, "If she has had a lot of money, she will expect you to provide for her in the same way."

Before anyone could even say anything else, Gordy said, "Nix that," and erased it.

When they finally finished, they had three things which they felt would encompass all other critical items. One, she had to be pretty. Two, she had to be nice. And three, she had to be a good mother.

As the boys looked at their list and thought about what they had decided were the most important qualities they wanted in a girl, I asked them the most important question of the lesson.

"And what are you doing to become the kind of man this kind of girl would be interested in?"

Standing Up for Someone

✦

I had just taught a Sunday lesson to my sixteen scouts about what to look for in a young lady, the kind they would like to marry. I finished by asking them what they were doing to become the type of young man that type of girl would be interested in. After class, the boys usually make a fast getaway, but instead, they hung around, whispering. That usually meant there was something more they wanted to discuss, so I took plenty of time gathering my books. Soon they came to me.

"Daris, could you help us with something?" Devin asked.

"If I can," I replied.

"Do you know Noelle?"

I nodded. "Of course."

Noelle was a very nice, pretty blonde girl that went to church with all of us.

Dallin joined the conversation. "The problem is, the guy she's dating is a jerk. He treats her like garbage."

Devin and Dallin were her brothers, so I asked if they had told their parents.

Dallin nodded. "Mom and Dad have talked to her, and so have the high school counselor and others, but she keeps going back to him."

"Have you ever stood up for her?" I asked.

"That's the problem," Devin said. "All of us want to, but we're sure she'd be annoyed."

"Why?" I asked.

"Her boyfriend is a senior, and he's big and strong," Mort answered. "And Noelle is a junior. We're just freshmen, and all of the older kids act like we're stupid. So we think if we interfere she'll be mad. Besides, he could beat any of us up."

Having worked with youth for some time, I learned was that young people can often do for each other what adults cannot.

"You know, boys," I said, "Over the years, I've learned that nice girls like Noelle seldom date jerks unless they think that's the best they can do. I bet no boy has ever told her she's better than that, and she would welcome knowing that you feel she is. As for her boyfriend, most bullies only pick on people weaker than themselves, but together all of you are strong."

"Then you don't think it would bother her if we told her boyfriend to treat her better?" Dallin asked.

"Not at all," I replied.

The boys went off, talking among themselves. A few weeks went by, and I had almost forgotten our conversation. Then, one day after church, Noelle came to me.

"Mr. Howard, I want to tell you something. I'm sure the boys won't tell you what they did, but I think you should know. One day at school, Mike, my boyfriend, was being mean. One of your scouts, my brother Devin, yelled at Mike to leave me alone.

"I was afraid Mike would beat him up, and he even grabbed Devin. When I told Mike to leave Devin alone, he told me to mind my own business. Then he picked Devin clear off the ground.

"Mike said, 'Are you tough enough to make me, little freshmen?' I started to cry, thinking Devin was going to really be hurt, and Mike told me to shut up. Devin said he wasn't tough enough to make him, and Mike sneered at him, saying, 'So who's going to?'

"Suddenly, there were fourteen more of your scouts there. One of them said, 'We will.'

"Mike looked around the circle and knew they meant it. One of them couldn't beat him, but all fifteen of them easily could. Mike set Devin back down and said, 'Perhaps I was wrong.' Devin snapped, 'There's no "perhaps" about it,' and Mike quickly walked away.

"I told Mike afterwards that I want nothing more to do with him." She started to cry as she continued. "If those boys feel I'm worth standing up for, I don't need a jerk like Mike."

Noelle said the boys told her I had talked to them about it. The boys never did tell me what they had done, but I couldn't help but feel proud of them and think to myself, "Great job, guys."

Tilling Service

⟡

I have a big tiller that will rip deep into the ground yet is small enough to load into my pickup. In the springtime, I try to take a few evenings and do some service tilling up garden spots for as many people as I can. Because I want my children to learn to serve, I often take them with me.

My aunt Thelma called me one spring. "Daris," she said, "your mother told me that you have a big tiller and would be willing to come till my garden."

"I'd be happy to," I replied.

"I haven't used my garden for a few years," she said. "I've spent the last couple of summers visiting family. The garden has a lot of grass in it. Will your tiller cut through that?"

"Easily," I answered.

"How much do you charge?" she asked.

When I explained that I liked to do it as service, I could just sense the frown on her face. I come from a family where the members are proud and insist on paying their way through life.

"We'll see," Aunt Thelma simply replied. "Do you remember where I live?"

I remembered well the many family gatherings at Aunt Thelma's house when I was a boy. My aunts were all good cooks, and Thelma was one of the best. The food was always incredibly delicious, and I always ate until I couldn't hold anymore.

On the appointed evening, I loaded my tiller into the back of my pickup, and my daughter joined me for the work. We drove the twenty miles to Aunt Thelma's house, and while I unloaded the tiller, my daughter went to tell her we were there.

I started the tiller and drove it to the backyard. Aunt Thelma met me at the edge of the garden and indicated the boundaries. A load of manure had been spread on it, but the ground, unused for a few years, had the consistency of cement. I tilled it north to south and then east to west, and then did it all over again. By the time I finished tilling, the soil was fluffy and nice.

Meanwhile, my daughter had been raking grass and rocks out of the soil the tiller had turned up. When I finished tilling, I grabbed a second rake and joined her. By the time we were done, the garden was clean, neat, and ready to plant. My daughter and I were both sweating, but we were pleased with the job we had done. As we were standing there looking at it, Aunt Thelma joined us.

"It's beautiful," she said. "Surely you will let me pay you for your work?"

"Aunt Thelma," I replied, "I don't let anyone pay for tilling. It's my way of giving back to family, friends, and the community. It's also how I teach my children to serve."

She smiled. "I thought you might say that. So I made you some popcorn balls. You won't turn them down, will you?"

Aunt Thelma made the best popcorn balls in the world. The homemade caramel melted in your mouth. Whenever there was a community food sale, her huge popcorn balls were always priced at about five dollars each, and they were the first to sell.

I laughed. "There is no way I will turn down your popcorn balls."

My daughter went with Aunt Thelma to get them while I loaded the tiller. Once it was loaded, I climbed into the pickup. There sat my daughter with three grocery bags full of popcorn balls, one popcorn ball half-eaten in her hand. I had assumed there would be a small bag with a half dozen at most.

"Dad, these are the best popcorn balls ever!"

"Three bags of them?"

My daughter nodded. "She gave us four or five dozen. She said she knew you wouldn't take the pay, so she made enough to make up for it. If you ever come till Aunt Thelma's garden again, you can count me in."

I laughed. I don't know that I taught my daughter about service that day, but working for popcorn balls is good, too.

Chariots of Tire

+

Hailee loved her job working at the nursing home, but she had one major challenge. That challenge went by the name of Bob.

Hailee could handle cleanups, spills, and even the sometimes impatient older people, but Bob's problem was altogether different. He didn't want to sleep until he was absolutely exhausted. So most nights, after all the work was wrapped up and all of the other patients were trying to sleep, Bob was noisily rolling up and down the halls in his wheelchair.

Hailee didn't know what to do. She had tried bribery. She had tried coaxing, begging, and everything else she could think of, but Bob refused to sleep. Putting him into his bed did no good; he would just climb back into his wheelchair. Confiscating his wheelchair wasn't an option because it was his own personal property.

"I wish we could figure a way to tire him out," one of the other staff members groaned.

Suddenly, Hailee had an idea. She checked with the doctor to make sure Bob's heart was strong enough, and then she approached Bob.

"Bob, how would you like to race me?"

Bob wheeled his chair around to face her. "As if that would be fair! You've got two good legs, and I'm stuck in this stupid wheelchair!"

"What if I got myself a wheelchair?" Hailee asked.

Many of the staff gathered around as it dawned on them what Hailee was doing. The halls were more than two wheelchairs wide, so there was plenty of space for racing.

Bob looked at her defiantly. "You wouldn't have a chance. I'm far more experienced than you are."

"Well, let's find out," Hailee said.

One of the other staff members quickly located a wheelchair. They brought it to the hallway just outside Bob's door. Hailee laid down a starting line across the carpet with masking tape.

"How far do you want to go?" she asked.

Bob laughed. "Let's make the whole loop. That is, if you think you have the strength. I'll even give you the inside track."

The nursing home was built in somewhat of a circular shape, with a big center courtyard. The loop would be about seventy yards. Hailee hadn't propelled herself along in a wheelchair that much before, but she didn't think it could be that hard.

She climbed into her chair and wheeled it up beside Bob, who was already sitting at the line ready to go. Another employee gave the signal, and they were off. Bob jumped to a quick lead, and no matter how hard Hailee tried, she fell farther and farther behind. Not long after she turned the last corner, she saw Bob pulling up to a stop at his door. When she pulled up beside him, he grinned. "Want to try again?"

She did, and he beat her by even more. After a third race he felt glorious in his victories, but he was tired and ready to sleep.

The next day, Hailee was sore and wasn't sure she could do it all again, even though Bob kept badgering her about another race. The other staffers, all happy that Bob slept more, encouraged her to take the challenge. With weary trepidation, she climbed into her designated wheelchair again that evening.

Hailee was farther behind than ever in the first race. But with her muscles warmed up, she shortened the gaps in the second and third rounds and gave Bob better competition than she had the previous day.

It became a big event in the nursing home after that. The other patients refused to have their doors shut until after the race each night so they could cheer as the two competitors sped past their doors. As the distances between Bob and Hailee continued to decrease, Bob began watching the chariot races from *Ben Hur* for motivation. But on the day that Hailee was sure she could at least tie with him, she received some bad news as she came to work. Bob had suddenly and unexpectedly passed away. As he was departing this life, he had spoken a message for her that the day shift employees had written down. They gave her the note.

She smiled through her tears as she read, "Hailee, you had better keep practicing so you're ready for a heavenly wheelchair race when you come."

A Good Horse

✛

My dad had trained our horse well. He had used Annie in the rodeo, for racing, and for just about everything else a horse could do. The problem was that sometimes she seemed too smart. My dad used to throw me on her back and say, "Just show her which cow you want and then hang on." More than once when she was chasing a cow, I had fallen off only to have Annie take the cow back to the barn without me.

"If I was ever in trouble, I'd take Annie over a dozen good men," Dad told me.

"But she left me in the pasture," I complained.

"That's because she was doing her job and knew you were okay," my dad replied.

I still had my doubts. I figured she would just leave me if things got tough.

I grew older and became a much better horseman. I could stick with Annie chasing cows around brush, over ditches, under trees, and just about anywhere.

But one day I was bringing the cows down from the upper pasture when one cow spooked and took off. She ran across the pasture at full tilt, and Annie and I were immediately after her. Along the opposite edge of the pasture was a ditch with lots of large trees growing beside it. On the other side of the ditch was sage brush.

We approached the ditch at a full gallop and were right on the cow's tail. The cow was moving so fast I was sure she would jump the ditch. But at the last minute, she turned under the trees. Annie turned, and I turned with her, but a branch caught me hard in the forehead and swept me from Annie's back.

I hit the ground, and the wind was knocked out of me. My head was spinning and hurt terribly. Then I heard a sound that sent a chill through me. It was bellowing from our bull. He was usually a very gentle, docile animal, but if he thought anyone was messing with his cows, he could be quite obnoxious.

I was able to sit up just enough to see that he was pawing the ground and looking in my direction. I realized he felt that the little chase we had was my fault and that I was bothering his cow. Annie was still in hot pursuit of her target, and I was left alone.

I tried to stand to move behind a tree, but when I did, the world seemed to spin, and I fell. With one last snort, the bull charged. I tried once more to stand only to fall again. I decided to crawl. The bull was coming fast, and I knew I couldn't make it to the tree in time.

The bull was almost on top of me when suddenly, Annie was there. She whirled and lashed out with her back feet, catching the bull hard in the shoulder, causing him to stumble. He immediately came back to his feet and ran out about fifty yards. Annie stepped in between him and me. The bull turned, tossed his head a couple of times, and then charged again.

Annie stood still, unflinching, as he pounded toward us. She seemed to be expertly waiting. Then, just at the right instant, she whirled and smashed her back feet into the side of his head. He crashed to the ground, sliding for a good distance. I was almost hit by both Annie's flying hooves and the bull's huge body when he landed.

My brain cleared a little, and I was able to move a distance away in case the bull decided to attack again. But this time he only bellowed his threats as he hurried back to the safety of the herd.

Annie stood patiently over me until I recovered enough balance to stand. I climbed onto her back and just held on while she herded the cows down to the lower pasture with no direction from me. When we reached the corral, my dad saw my bruised, swollen forehead and my blackened eyes, and he hurried over to help me down.

"We need to get you to the house," he said.

I nodded. "But I think we need to give Annie an extra helping of oats first."

A Supercharged Battery

$\div$

My high school mechanics teacher assigned team captains by our grades on the book work. Sam had the highest score and was assigned to the first team. I had the second highest score and was assigned as head of team two. Four more boys were also assigned as team captains. The other thirty-nine boys were distributed to the six teams based on grades. But we quickly learned that good book-work grades did not necessarily translate to excellence in doing actual mechanic work.

Our teacher had six engines, one for each team. He "bugged" the engines so they wouldn't start. These bugs could be as simple as draining all the gas from the tank or as complicated as replacing good wires with bad ones, which looked fine on the outside but were dead inside and didn't carry electricity.

We continued to learn new things each week, but Friday was our favorite day. Every Friday, our teacher would go through each engine, doing the same hacks to each one, and then we would race to see which team could get their engine running first.

I learned that often, the team members who struggled to pass tests on classroom work did the best job on the engines. I determined the strengths of each team member and assigned them to that specialty. We all helped each other, but each person was in charge of their own area, and the rest of the team deferred to them on it. With that strategy, my team always had any hacked engine running in less than ten minutes.

Sam, on the other hand, drove his team crazy. He felt he knew more than anybody and insisted on making all the decisions, only letting his team make suggestions.

On one particular competition day, our engine was cranking but did not fire. Our team member specializing in the fuel system and carburetor assured us there was fuel getting to the cylinders. Our spark plug expert found no spark there. I took apart the distributor and tested the rotor and capacitor, which was my specialty. The capacitor was bad. We switched it out for a new one, and our engine fired up immediately.

Sam's team determined similar things, but instead of checking to see if something was wrong inside the distributor, Sam insisted the engine wasn't cranking fast enough.

Riley, one of Sam's team members, said, "That's crazy! The engine cranks fine." But Sam decided he knew better. He pulled over two battery chargers, connected them to the battery, and turned them both to the highest boost setting.

Riley, who was testing the electrical system on the engine, had turned his back to Sam. Our team had our backs to him as well. But I smelled something and heard sizzling. I turned and saw the two chargers connected to the battery, with acid bubbling out of the holes on top.

"Get away!" I yelled.

We dashed away and so did all of Sam's team except for Riley, who was still bent over the engine. We had barely moved to a safe distance when the battery exploded. A wave of battery acid hit Riley from the back.

We immediately hauled him over to the emergency shower. Even though he had on full-length coveralls, his clothes underneath were wet from both acid and water, and he was mad.

Riley started yelling at Sam and was threatening him with bodily harm when the class bell rang. Sam took off running to his next class. Riley jerked off his coveralls, threw them on his hook, and ran after Sam.

I stayed with a few of the others to help clean up, and by the time we finished, we had missed most of our next class. As I hung up my coveralls next to Riley's, I bumped his, and the whole back of them peeled away and fell to the floor. We all gasped and looked at each other.

Knowing the acid may have soaked through to Riley's clothes, our teacher said, "I think it might be good if one of you told Riley about this. Immediately!"

An Acidic Situation

✦

In our mechanics class, Sam had attached two powerful chargers to a battery that was already fully charged, blowing it apart and sending a stream of acid down Riley's back. We flooded Riley and his clothes in the emergency shower, finishing just as the end-of-class bell rang. He threw his coveralls on the hook and chased Sam out the door as Sam ran to his next class to get away.

As a group of us finished cleaning up the mess, I bumped Riley's coveralls, and the whole back of them fell apart. Our teacher, afraid that the acid might also have soaked into Riley's clothes, told us to quickly find Riley and warn him.

We had been so long cleaning that the next class hour was almost over. As we left the mechanics shop, there was a bit of joking.

"Hey," Lenny said, "maybe we shouldn't tell him and see what happens."

"You don't think his clothes would fall apart like his coveralls did, do you?" Tom asked.

"For Riley's sake, I hope not," I answered.

"And for the sake of anyone who might see him," Lenny joked.

"Does anyone know what class Riley has second hour?" I asked.

We all looked back and forth at each other, but everyone just shrugged and shook their heads, so we stopped at the office. The secretary looked at the five of us suspiciously.

"Why aren't you in class?" she asked. I explained how we had stayed to clean up the acid. "Okay," she replied, "I will verify that with your teacher. Now, hurry to class."

"We have one more thing we have to do," I said. "But we need to know what class Riley is in."

She gave us another suspicious look and asked why, so I explained the situation.

"All right," she said. "I will look up his information. But I don't think it takes all of you to warn him. The rest of you can go to class."

The others left the office while I got the information. The secretary told me that Riley was currently in Mrs. Eddington's Spanish class. I thanked her and headed on my way. As I stepped out of the office, the others were waiting for me.

"I thought you were all heading to your classes," I said.

Lenny laughed. "Are you crazy? We wouldn't miss this for the world. If the acid did soak through the coveralls, we want to be there to see what happens."

We arrived at Mrs. Eddington's classroom only a minute before the next class bell rang. We looked in and saw Riley sitting in his seat, bored and slouching.

"Well," Lenny said, "it looks like his clothes are still intact."

Just then the bell rang, and the students started gathering their books. We thought we would simply wait outside the classroom and talk to Riley when he came out, but we didn't get the chance. Riley stretched and stood, and when he did, the back of his clothes stayed on the chair. His backside was completely bare from just below his shoulders down to his ankles.

Riley turned to see what everyone was gasping at. As he did, he exposed his backside to Mrs. Eddington. Mrs. Eddington, a big, older woman whom the students affectionately called "Mom," gasped. In an instant, she took her big coat from the hook near her desk, and in three giant leaps she bounded across the room and tackled Riley, throwing her coat around him.

"Well," Lenny said, "I don't think we need to warn him anymore. I think he just figured it out."

Flowers Don't Last Forever

✦

Looking out the window, my wife, Donna, saw two little girls. Both were about nine years old and from single-parent homes. Each of them had recently struggled through some tough situations. We had watched these little girls, who were already quite shy, turn even more inward.

Donna has a beautiful flower garden that was in full bloom with tulips, daffodils, hyacinths, and many other flowers. The girls had been walking down our road and stopped to enjoy the array of colors. The flowers were too tempting, and the girls decided to walk into the middle of them. Alean couldn't help herself and picked a flower. Becky leaned down to follow suit when she glanced at our big picture window and saw Donna standing there. Instead of picking the flower, Becky waved innocently.

Donna smiled and waved back, and since she was planning to leave anyway, she took her stuff out to the car so she could visit with the girls. As she did, Alean slid behind a tree and guiltily dropped the flower she had picked.

"Do you like my flowers?" Donna asked.

Becky nodded enthusiastically. "They're very pretty!"

"Well, they're not going to last forever," Donna replied. "I think you should each take one home. What do you think?"

Each girl smiled, nodded, and then each picked her favorite flower. They happily carried their flowers home to put them in some water.

Over the next few weeks, Donna saw the girls return multiple times. Often they would pick a flower and then head back home with it. But more and more Donna could tell the girls were hanging around, hoping she would come out.

Donna would come out of the house and invite the girls to sit in the shade of the deck. There they would talk as they enjoyed the porch swings. Donna had a million things to do: papers to grade, dishes to wash, and floors to sweep. But she knew that these little girls needed more friendly adults in their lives, so she put it all aside to visit. On these occasions, Donna didn't do much other than listen.

When I came home from work one day, Donna told me about the girls. I was reminded of when I first put in the flower garden many years earlier. It was still early in the spring of that year. I had mulched it, tilled it, put in a sprinkling system, and finally planted the early spring bulbs.

It seemed like it took forever for the flowers to come, but they finally did. We had a full rainbow of colors from red tulips to yellow daffodils to blue hyacinths. I was proud of it.

Then one day, as I came in from working outside, I saw through the window my young children marching into the house with arm loads of flowers. I looked past them and saw that the beautiful flower garden was nothing but a mass of stems. The only color it contained was green.

Our children walked into the house with huge smiles on their faces. Donna joined me, and when she saw the flower garden, she gasped. But as each child delivered an armful of flowers to us, along with a hug, my heart felt warm within me.

As the children went back outside to play, Donna turned to me and said, "Flowers don't last forever, anyway."

My mind returned to the present as Donna finished telling me the story of the little girls.

I looked at our increasingly bare flower garden as she said once again, "Flowers don't last forever, anyway."

I thought again of my children, now grown, whom I miss having at home. I nodded and thought, "Neither does childhood."

Hugs

✦

The director of the nursing home called an urgent staff meeting. He had a perplexing problem, and he wasn't sure what to do. In addition, the entire staff would need to implement the decision.

"The reason I have called this meeting," he told the staff, "is that John Samuelson, the new man in Room 132, goes around hugging everyone. Why, this morning, I had no sooner stepped into the nursing home than he hugged me."

John was the youngest man in the nursing home and the newest resident there. He had been a happy, vibrant man, full of energy, love of life, and love of people. Then an automobile accident left him with some major brain damage. No longer able to take care of himself, he had come to the nursing home. But the wonderful traits of his personality were not squelched by his new challenges. Instead, his sense of social normalcy was destroyed, and his big heart became abundantly evident.

"But John doesn't hug anyone in a bad way," Amy, one of the staff members, replied. "He just can't help himself. He loves everyone."

"Yeah," David said. "John's love and happiness are contagious. He's lifted the spirit of everyone here, the staff and residents alike. I don't think there's a person here who doesn't enjoy his daily hugs."

Ellen added her view. "I know I like his hugs. And most people in this place have little to look forward to. Everyone I have talked to says that his daily hug brightens their day."

The director didn't budge. "I'm positive that sooner or later we're going to get a complaint. All we need is just one lady who thinks John is getting fresh, and we'll have a lawsuit on our hands."

"But how can you tell John not to hug people?" Amy says. "It would devastate him."

"I don't want to hurt John's feelings," the director said, "but the welfare of the patients and this facility has to come first."

"I think John's hugs are good for the welfare of everyone," David countered.

"But it's what the residents think that matters," the director said.

"I have an idea," Ellen said. "Maybe Anna could call a meeting of the residents and find out how they feel."

Anna was an older, no-nonsense lady who had appointed herself head of all the residents, forming what she called "the Resident Council." At times, she would call a meeting in the main living room, and they would decide what they did and didn't like about how things were being run. She would then pass that information to the director and the staff, and she never let anyone rest until things were corrected according to the group's decision.

The director was reluctant to get Anna involved in this issue because he knew once her group made a decision, he would never hear the end of it. But he finally agreed he should seek their input. Ellen was tasked with talking to Anna. By the next day, Anna had called a meeting to get a consensus on what everyone thought of John's hugs.

The day after the meeting, Anna delivered a written note to the staff and the director indicating the decision of the Resident Council. On the outside of the note was written the words, "By unanimous consent of the Resident Council." The staff all gathered around to see what the note said. Written inside were just four words to the director and staff, succinctly and clearly stating how the residents felt.

"Mind your own business."

Thus John continued his daily hugs for everyone.

Key Comments

I finished passing my students back their graded linear algebra exams.

"Check the tests over," I told them. "Make sure the points I gave you add up to the score listed. Let me know if you have any questions or if there's anything you disagree with."

David raised his hand. "You really want us to talk to you about our tests?"

"Yes," I replied. "If you want to. I finished grading these at about midnight last night, and with forty of you, I was quite brain dead when I finished. I might have made mistakes."

"What if we find some grading we disagree with?" he asked.

"Then you should definitely come talk to me about it. If you can show me something I missed, or if you can make a case for how you understood the problem differently from what I thought, then I may give you some more points. I may also disagree with you, but even if I do, I feel it is your right to visit with me about it."

David seemed surprised by this, and he stood off to the side as three students formed in a line to visit with me after class. The first student showed that I had added the points wrong. He received one more point. The second student pointed out a problem where his work continued onto the back of a page, which I hadn't seen when I graded it. He earned two more points. The third thought some work was correct, but it wasn't, so his grade didn't change.

David waited patiently until all of the others were done, and then he approached me.

"You actually did mean we could talk to you if we had problems with the test, didn't you?"

"Of course," I replied. "Why does that surprise you?"

"My math teacher in high school wouldn't let us talk about the test or ask questions or anything, even after it was all graded."

"I feel a test is a good way to learn," I replied. "People often learn more from their mistakes than from their successes."

"My high school teacher didn't believe that," David said. "We were hardly allowed to breathe while taking a test. One day our teacher passed out the test we were taking and set them upside down on our desks. We weren't allowed to say anything from the minute he started passing them out. We all sat there quietly until everyone had one. Then, at the given signal, we turned our tests over.

"After we turned our tests over, I looked at mine and then raised my hand. The teacher yelled at me. 'David, what did I tell you? I told you that you were not to speak or raise your hand from the minute I started passing out the test, didn't I?' He continued to yell at me for about five minutes, and when I tried to say something, he just got madder and yelled louder.

"Finally, he yelled, 'Just do your test, and we will talk afterward!' So that's what I did."

"What was your question?" I asked.

"That's the fun part," David replied. "It wasn't a question. It was a statement. When everyone had completed their tests, and our teacher had gathered them, he turned to me and angrily asked, 'So, David, what was so important that made you think you didn't have to follow a few simple rules?'"

David grinned as he finished the story. "I told him, 'The test you put on my desk was the answer key.'"

A Neighbor Enemy

✦

On Memorial Day 2012, Fred and his friend Akio visited Camp Minidoka. As Fred read the words on the memorial there, a lot of memories flooded into his heart. He remembered the dismay he felt when his new neighbors moved in. They were different from him, and he didn't like different. He didn't view himself as prejudiced, but he was not open to anyone who was not like himself.

Although the new neighbors tried to initiate a friendship, Fred did not return their kindness. Soon their overtures faded, and each family kept to themselves. Then, on December 7, 1941, everything changed overnight. Japan bombed Pearl Harbor, and Fred could no longer tolerate such people as neighbors. They were Japanese, so they were the enemy. The nation declared war, Fred's oldest son, Brian, was drafted, and Fred's animosity and suspicion of his neighbors grew.

Only a couple of months after the bombing of Pearl Harbor, President Roosevelt signed a law to move people like Fred's neighbors into internment camps. Fred was relieved. No longer would he have to worry about them possibly causing trouble. He watched with satisfaction as they quickly prepared to move. Fred purchased their house for a minimal amount, determined to carefully control who could move in as his neighbors in the future.

The Japanese internment camp where they were taken was a hundred miles away. Despite the government's assurances that conditions in the camps were good, word spread that their food was low quality and in low supply, and that conditions, in general, were less than ideal. Some churches united in humanitarian efforts to offer relief, but Fred turned away those who asked him to participate. Surely the admonition to "love thy enemy" did not pertain to times of war.

The months rolled into years, and Fred received word that Brian had been wounded fighting in Europe. Though still alive, Brian's wounds were severe enough that he would be sent home. Fred waited anxiously for the day of his son's return. Finally, Fred received a phone call from New York.

"Dad," Brian said, "I'm coming home, and I'm bringing a friend."

The whole family was at the station at the appointed time. When the train stopped, Fred anxiously searched the disembarking crowd for his son. Fred spotted Brian at about the same moment everyone else in the family did, and they all rushed toward their returning soldier. But as they drew near, Fred pulled up sharply. There, next to his son, was a young Japanese man in an American army uniform. Fred noticed that Brian was missing a leg, and the Japanese man was missing an arm.

Brian smiled at his father. "Dad, you remember our neighbor Kim Sato, don't you?"

The young Japanese man reached out his left hand, the only one he had, but Fred remained stiff. Then Brian's next words burned through Fred's soul as nothing had before.

"Dad, I'm alive today because of Kim. I fell wounded on the battlefield, and Kim crawled out and pulled me to safety, losing his arm and nearly losing his life."

Fred slowly took Kim's extended hand, and as he did, he stuttered, "But you are Japanese."

Kim looked directly into Fred's eyes and said, "I am an American, same as you."

The gamut of emotion flooding into Fred's heart was so intense he could hardly fathom it. His feelings ranged from the shame of not even knowing his neighbor's name to deep gratitude for his son's safe return.

From then on, Fred did all he could to help those in the internment camp, even making personal visits and taking food. He became friends with Akio, Kim's father, and when the day came that the Sato family was allowed to return home, Fred was there to welcome them.

In 2012, Fred and Akio were visiting Camp Minidoka assisted by their sons. They came to see the new memorial that had been built in honor of those from the camp who had faithfully served their country, even while their own families were interned there based solely on their ancestry. As Fred read Franklin D. Roosevelt's words on the memorial, he felt they said it all:

"Americanism is a matter of the mind and heart. Americanism is not, and never was, a matter of race or ancestry."

Putting Down a Deposit

✦

Gary and Richard were neighbors and best friends. It also happened that each of them had had his first child born at nearly the same time, and both children were girls. So when those girls approached dating age, it was natural for the two men to compare notes as to how they would handle the situation.

"At least the first time each boy comes to pick up my daughter, I plan to make sure that I will be cleaning my shotgun so he knows I mean business," Richard said.

"I considered that," Gary said, "but it's so old-fashioned. I think I've come up with a better, more modern approach."

"What's that?" Richard asked.

"I'm going to make the boy put down a deposit. If he brings my daughter home safe, sound, and on time, he will get his deposit back. If he doesn't, he loses it. In addition, if he lost his deposit and he wants to ask her out again, the deposit will double the next time."

Richard thought Gary's approach was interesting, but he said he would stick with cleaning his shotgun.

The girls started dating, and each father carried out his plan. Richard's shotgun convinced the boys to be considerate of his daughter. On the other hand, Gary started the first deposit at one hundred dollars. This kept most boys in line. However, one or two ended up losing their deposit when they didn't get her home at the proper hour. These boys never asked her out again since they decided two hundred dollars was too high.

Gary's daughter, Sally, didn't like it. She felt it was controlling and demeaning. But Gary thought it was good. If the boy didn't plan to get her home on time, he shouldn't ask her out. And if she wasn't worth the deposit, then Gary felt the boy didn't value her enough to treat her well.

Time went on, and after high school Sally was still living at home while attending college, so her father kept the same rules in place. She met a young man named Carl. He was fond of Sally and asked her out. Carl put down the deposit, and when brought Sally home on time, Gary offered the deposit back.

Carl laughed. "Just put it toward the next date."

Things went well for quite a while, and then, one night, Carl brought Sally home almost half an hour late. Sally explained that they had a flat tire on the way home, but the reason didn't matter. Gary kept the deposit. It took Carl a little while to get two hundred dollars, but soon he was dating Sally again. Just as before, he kept putting the deposit toward the next date.

Then came the day that Carl brought Sally home late again. Gary didn't give the deposit back, and Sally complained.

"But, Dad, we were in the middle of a serious talk about marriage."

Gary liked Carl, but he said a deal was a deal and still refused to return the deposit. "But what if I end up marrying her?" Carl asked. "Do I get all of my deposits back then?"

"We'll cross that bridge when we come to it," Gary said.

Carl came up with four hundred dollars and continued to date Sally. But that wasn't the last time he ended up getting her home late. There were two more. Sally tried to talk her father out of the deposit each time, but to no avail.

"If you are worth it to him, he will find a way," Gary said.

It took Carl a while to come up with eight hundred dollars. When it came to the sixteen hundred dollars, Carl sold his motorcycle.

"Sally and I had better get married soon or I'll be broke," he said.

Happily, it wasn't too long before Sally and Carl were engaged. When the wedding day came, the young couple approached Gary about getting the deposits back. Gary smiled but shook his head.

"I thought about it, and I think it was a good lesson for you to learn."

But then Carl said something that made Gary rethink his strategy and helped him also understand more how Sally felt about it.

Carl, with a smile, said, "And I have learned the lesson well. I told Sally we should start with a one hundred dollar deposit on each child when you want to take your grandchildren somewhere, with it doubling each time you get them home late."

Gary gave the deposits back, and Sally's sisters were spared their father's "modern" dating controls.

A Perfect Advantage

✦

Samuel was a perfectionist. He always had been. His bedroom had to be perfect. His clothes were aligned in the drawers. His books were shelved so the spines formed an exact line. And everything else had to be perfect. Needless to say, he drove everyone crazy.

Then Samuel got drafted into the army. There his perfectionist attitude hit its zenith. The army demanded of its soldiers that everything be perfect, but few ever succeeded. Samuel found that the military and his perfectionism were made for each other. After a long weekend out on drill, most of the men would get a drink to wind down. Samuel would head back to his barracks to organize his foot locker, align the blankets on his bed, and fix anything else that wasn't exactly right.

At every inspection, the commanding officers found something wrong with everyone—everyone, that is, except Samuel. They tried in every way to find just one thing wrong with Samuel's uniform, bed, locker, personal grooming, or anything else, but they never could—at least, not without making something up and making themselves look stupid. Even the general, who was the camp commander, tried at one inspection, but he found nothing. After a few more desperate attempts, they gave up.

Then one day, Samuel received word that his grandfather had passed away. He was sure a request for leave to attend the funeral would be denied. The officers had never granted such a request for anyone. Still, Samuel decided he would try.

As he approached the officer's quarters, the windows were open due to the summer heat, and Samuel couldn't help overhearing the voices inside. The commanding general was especially animated.

"I tell you, Private Hadderson is not normal!" the general said. Samuel was surprised to hear them talking about him.

"In what way?" a captain asked.

"No lowly private is that perfect," the general said. "I'm sure he's only pretending to be a private."

"Why would anyone in their right mind pretend to be a private?" a major asked.

"It's obvious," the general replied. "He's a spy from headquarters. I've seen it before. They get word of abuse in the camp and send someone to play the part of the lowly private. He does everything perfectly to make us hate him, expecting us to heap abuse on him so he'll have something to report against us."

"So what do we do?" the captain asked.

"We won't fall for it," the general replied. "We'll act like he's a private, but we'll make sure we are kind and considerate."

"But what if we're wrong?" the major asked. "What if he is just a private?"

"It will be easy to figure out," the general replied. "Sooner or later, he'll need to return and report to headquarters. He'll come up with some excuse to go on leave. If he does, we'll know for sure he's a spy."

"But we never grant leaves for anything," the captain said. "We'll just deny the request."

"Are you stupid?" the general replied. "Then he would have something against us."

Samuel thought this might be a good time to enter the building. He told the secretary about his grandfather's passing and expressed his desire for a leave. She said she would pass a note to Samuel's commanding officer who was in the meeting.

A few minutes later, it was not Samuel's commanding officer but the general who came out to greet him. As Samuel saluted, the general smiled broadly and exchanged all-knowing glances with the other officers.

"So you want a leave to go to your grandfather's funeral?" the general asked.

"Yes, sir," Samuel replied. "Just for three days."

"We like to be understanding," the general said. "Why don't you take a week?"

And Samuel did.

Good Pay

✦

Just before school let out for the summer, a middle school teacher asked if I would be willing to speak to her class. I love to visit with young people and happily accepted.

"Would you mind bringing some books?" she asked. "We have read three of your stories in class this year, and there are quite a few children who would like to buy books and have you sign them."

Of course, I was happy to do that.

The day arrived for me to visit the school. I decided to leave the books in the car, except for a few to show while I spoke to the children. I decided I would return for the other books later once I knew how many were needed.

The presentation was fun. The children loved the books and had lots of questions. Each child told me his or her favorite part, and they all wanted to know when my next book would be out.

During our visit, one little boy caught my eye. His clothes were somewhat ragged and didn't fit him well. His hair was uncombed, and he had a rather defiant attitude. He didn't ask as many questions as the others, but when he did ask, he had an intensity that told me that he had lived the stories when the class had read them.

As we finished our discussion, the teacher took count of which students wanted to buy books. Almost every student wanted at least one. But once more, my attention was drawn to the little boy with the ragged clothes. He approached his teacher with some apprehension.

"May I go call my mother and see if I can get some money to buy a book?" he asked.

The teacher shook her head. "Daniel, you know I can't let you go to the office. You're on the no-call list."

Daniel pleaded for a short time, but when the answer remained the same, he suddenly took off out of the classroom. The teacher sent her aide after him and then turned to me to explain.

"Daniel hates school and doesn't do well. He uses the excuse to call home to sneak away and leave, so the school put him on the no-call list."

"Why does he hate school?" I asked.

"No matter how hard we try to help him, he doesn't want to learn. He also struggles to make friends."

"That's what the one book is about," I said.

She nodded. "In so many ways, it's Daniel's story. While we read it, he was totally enthralled. That's unusual for him because we can't get him to do much with books. After we had finished it as a class, I think he read it twice on his own. It's the only book he's read all year. But even if he called home, his parents wouldn't buy it for him. They don't think reading has any value. Their attitude is probably why Daniel doesn't like school."

She handed me the list, and I went out to my van to bring in the books. As I did, I thought about my own experience in school as a boy. Although the book Daniel liked is fiction, much of it is based on my own experiences. As I gathered the books the students had requested, I put one extra into the box.

On my way back to the classroom, I passed the principal and the teacher's aide. They were having little success talking Daniel into returning to the classroom. When I handed the books to the teacher, she counted them.

"You have one more than we paid for," she said.

I nodded. "Is it okay if I leave it for Daniel?"

She smiled. "That would be wonderful. Maybe it will be what we need to break through the barrier he's built around himself."

A few days later, I was looking through the thank-you letters the students had written to me. One had almost unintelligible writing but had a well-drawn picture. It was from Daniel. There was also a note from the teacher. It simply said, "When I gave your book to Daniel, it was the first time I have seen him smile all year."

And I knew I had received good pay for that book.

Snakes

✦

Twelve-year-old Kevin loved to tease his fourteen-year-old sister, Sally. It helped that she was afraid of any critter that walked, crawled, or slithered. He was forever putting a rubber bug in her cereal, plastic spiders in her shoes, or Halloween eyeballs in her backpack, where they would pop out at her when she opened it.

When she was distracted, he loved to don the scariest mask he could find and sneak up on her. He would tap her on the shoulder, and when she turned to look at him, he would let out a wail that was immediately drowned out by Sally's shriek.

But the things Kevin loved most were rubber snakes. Kevin bought dozens of them. He put them everywhere. His favorite places to hide them were in the bathroom, in Sally's bed, and in her locker at school. Her locker was difficult. Sally was smart enough to protect her locker combination from him, so he had to sneak up on her after she had opened it. He knew she would eventually look down or turn to talk to someone. Then he would slip the snake over the open locker door.

The last time he pulled that trick, Sally turned back to her locker and screamed so loudly that some of the other students dropped to the floor in fear, thinking the school was under attack. She was teased mercilessly for the rest of the day until she was totally humiliated. Sally was determined to steel herself against Kevin's pranks so he wouldn't have the joy of hearing her scream again.

But Kevin had his own troubles. His actions landed him in the principal's office, and his parents were contacted. They told him they had had enough. He was informed that he was grounded for a week, and if he ever pranked Sally again, it would be for longer. Kevin promised that his pranks on Sally would end.

Sally, however, was not aware of Kevin's promise, nor was Kevin aware of Sally's commitment. And neither of them could know that fate still had a hand to play.

When Kevin was walking home from school, he happened to come upon a garden snake. Remembering that his science teacher had just set up a new snake terrarium, Kevin thought he would be a class hero by being the first one to bring a snake for it.

Kevin took off his shirt and used it to catch the snake. He proudly marched home with his catch, but when he got there, he realized his dilemma. Where was he going to put it?

He hunted for a bucket, but he couldn't find one that was tall enough. He searched for any container that would keep the snake safely enclosed, but there just wasn't anything available. Then Kevin had a brilliant idea. Since everyone showered in the mornings, he would just put the snake in the bathtub and warn everyone about it when the family gathered that evening.

Of course, fate wasn't done playing its hand. Sally was on a community girls' volleyball team, and she had a game after school. The hot water heater at the YMCA where they played happened to be broken. So Sally, along with most of the girls, decided they would wait until they got home to shower. The minute Sally arrived at her house, she went directly to the bathroom.

She undressed and opened the shower door into the bathtub. She saw the snake and almost screamed, but remembering her commitment, she was determined that no rubber snake would get the best of her again. She reached down and grabbed it to throw it out of the tub, but that snake did something no rubber snake had ever done. It lifted its head, looked at her, and flicked its tongue.

Luckily for Kevin, Sally had the presence of mind to grab a towel on her way out the door, otherwise his grounding would have been longer. As it was, he was only grounded for ten years.

Getting a Driver's License

+

Having been a deputy sheriff for a long time, Ted had learned that the minute he thought he had seen everything, something new came along. For that reason, he was not surprised by what happened in the sheriff's office that morning.

The office had hired an older woman, Lanna, as a part-time secretary. Lanna had grown up in a distant city, and she made it clear that she thought this small rural community was odd. Lanna was also a no-nonsense kind of woman, which is why the sheriff had decided that she would be the perfect addition to their office for the summer. The other secretaries wanted time off for family vacations, and Lanna would be the fill-in person.

During the school year, Lanna was a secretary at the high school, a position she had filled for as long as anyone could remember. Everyone in the office knew Lanna because she had been the secretary during the time they had all gone to high school. No one would consider crossing her—they all knew better. She had heard just about every possible excuse someone could make up, and she didn't put up with any of them.

Ted watched with great interest when Jake Allender walked into the office. Jake was fourteen, the youngest age at which a person could legally get a driver's license in their state. He lived on a farm thirty miles out of town. Summer was a very busy time for the Allenders, so Ted was surprised when Jake plopped his completed driving permit on the counter. Ted couldn't imagine anyone in Jake's family taking the time away from work to bring Jake in to get his license.

Ted could see that Lanna thought the same thing. She eyed Jake suspiciously as she spoke.

"May I help you?"

Jake nodded. "I finished driver's ed, and my father wants me to get my license so I can help drive trucks this summer."

"Where's your father?" Lanna asked.

"He's busy at home working."

"So who brought you in to get your license?" she questioned.

"I brought myself," Jake replied. "No one had time to bring me."

"Just as I thought," Lanna said. "Since you took driver's ed you obviously know that driving without an adult, when all you have is your permit is totally illegal. You do know that, don't you?"

"Well, yes, but . . ."

"And you know that if you're caught driving with only a permit, without an adult with you, that you can receive a ticket?"

"Yes, but . . ."

"And you do know, don't you, that if you get a ticket during the time you only have your learner's permit, you will not be able to get a license for another full year?"

"Yes, but . . ."

Lanna interrupted again and turned to Ted. "Deputy, I expect you to take this young man out to his car and give him a ticket."

Jake again started to complain. "But I didn't . . ."

Lanna interrupted him once more and pointed to the door. "Go with the deputy."

Jake sighed, turned, and walked outside with Ted. They soon returned.

"Did you give him a ticket?" Lanna asked.

Ted shook his head. "He hasn't broken the law."

"What do you mean he hasn't broken the law? He drove here, didn't he?"

Ted nodded. "Yes. On a tractor. He doesn't have to have a license to drive a tractor. It's parked right outside. You can see for yourself."

Lanna just shook her head, rolled her eyes, and said, "This is a weird town."

The Happiest Man on Earth

My daughter Trissa is a band and choir teacher for a small school district in Idaho. She and her students had worked hard to earn money to go to Disneyland. The students excitedly boarded the bus for their journey, and away they went. As could be expected with a lot of excited students, the trip included stops at almost every out-of-the-way place that had any semblance of a restroom.

They were out on a long stretch of road across the California desert, and Trissa was looking forward to a much-needed rest at the hotel, when she received the all-too-familiar information that someone needed to use the bathroom.

"Here?" Trissa asked. "In the middle of the desert?"

The bus driver rolled her eyes. "Maybe we can just pull over, and the person with the small bladder can water a cactus."

Perhaps if the bus hadn't been co-ed that might have been a good plan, but instead, they started looking for a place to pull off that might have a bathroom. Finally, a sign appeared that indicated there was a town only a half mile off of the highway that had "services."

The bus driver reluctantly pulled the bus onto the two-lane road that looked like it headed into the middle of nowhere. They followed it for a half mile and came to an old gas station with a couple of small shops. One was a hat shop.

Trissa thought it was strange to have a hat shop in the middle of nowhere, so while the students lined up at the bathrooms and purchased pop and candy, she went to the hat store. She wandered in and found hats of all types and sizes. She eventually found the store owner. After visiting with him for a minute, Trissa found him to be about the happiest person she had ever met. She wondered how he could be so happy. She was the only one in the store, and he obviously wasn't selling a lot of hats.

"You seem so happy," Trissa said to him. "Why?"

He laughed. "Why should I not be happy? I live in greatest country on earth."

"Did you live somewhere else previously?" she asked.

He nodded. "This desert remind me of it. That why stay here."

"So why did you leave?" Trissa asked. "You must have liked it if you settled in a similar place."

"The country where I live not free," he replied. "Government take away much. But when coming to take away family, I sell all I have and come to America. I have nothing left, but family safe, and we now American citizens."

"What country are you are from?" Trissa asked.

He shook his head. "It no matter. I not citizen of that country. I American. It now my country, and I have no other country."

"But you sold everything you had," Trissa said. "You can't make much selling hats here."

"It no matter," he replied. "I make little, raise food, and feed family. But most important, I still have family and be free. That more important than all things sold to come here."

Trissa found a pretty white summer hat and purchased it. She wore it out into the hot sun, and many of her students gathered around.

"Where did you get that awesome hat?" one girl asked.

"From the happiest man on earth," Trissa replied. "Maybe you should see if he has one you would like."

The man sold lots of hats that day, but Trissa knew that although he would appreciate the money, it was his family and freedom that truly made him happy.

Parking Plots

Mr. B. was a drivers' education teacher with a strong personality. Sometimes his attitude about certain driving things annoyed him enough that they would slip into his classroom discussions. Recently, something had really annoyed him.

"Do you want to know what almost gives me road rage?" he asked his drivers' education class.

"What?" Tim asked.

"When someone parks across the middle line between two parking stalls," Mr. B. answered.

Tim's twin brother, Jim, asked, "What do you mean?"

"Let me show you the one that annoys me the most," Mr. B. replied.

He put a picture up on the screen. It showed a big, beautiful car parked across the center line between two parking spots.

"This lady," Mr. B. grumbled, "parks her car in this area every day, and she always parks right across the middle of two places."

"Why does she do that?" Tim asked.

"Most people do it to give room on both sides or ends of their car to keep it from being scratched. But it's selfish and takes a parking spot away from someone else. This lady parks there almost every morning, and her car is there all day."

"Isn't that illegal?" Jim asked.

Mr. B. shook his head. "Not in this town. But it ought to be. Quite often I've needed to park in that area, and there was nothing available, but there her car sat across two spots. I'd give a hundred dollars to anyone who could figure a way to teach her not to do that."

Mr. B. saw Jim and Tim glance at each other, so he added, "A legal way."

Every day during drivers' education, although Mr. B. fretted about his disgust for different things, he always returned to the subject of the lady that parked across two parking spots. When the students started practicing driving, Mr. B. often had them drive past the car that disgusted him. After they had finished drivers' education, Jim and Tim practiced their driving hours with their parents, looking forward to trading their learner's permits for real driver's licenses. The minute they had their licenses, they went to Mr. B.

"Is that hundred-dollar offer still available?" Tim asked.

"What do you have in mind?" Mr. B. asked.

After Jim and Tim had explained their plan, Mr. B. laughed and assured them that if they were able to do it, he'd pay.

The two boys went to their dad, who owned a used car lot. It took a little longer to convince him, but he finally agreed to their plan. Early the next morning, the two boys drove away in the two smallest compact cars their father had on his lot. They waited until the lady had parked her car across two spots as usual. Then, after she left, each of the brothers took turns pulling his car up so their bumpers were just inches from the one's of the lady's car. There was no way she could pull out of the parking spot. The little compact cars barely stayed within the lines of the parking spots, making it so there were three cars in the two spots. The two boys locked the cars and walked to school.

Three days later, the police called. Jim and Tim's dad passed the phone to them. The officer had a chuckle in his voice as he spoke.

"Would you mind removing your cars? Although it's legal for you to leave them there, the lady whose car you have hemmed in would like her car back, and she has promised she won't park that way again."

Jim and Tim removed the cars and became one hundred dollars richer.

Softball Mentality

＋

My wife called me in from working in the garden to take an urgent-sounding phone call. When I answered, I heard the voice of my neighbor, Mel.

"Daris," he said, "I understand that you used to pitch for our community softball team a few years back."

"More like a hundred years back," I replied. "Back in the time of the dinosaurs."

"Here's our problem," he said. "The only pitcher we have is out of town. We had a lot of guys try to pitch at practice last night, and frankly, they stunk. The balls were too high, too low, inside, and outside—but never in the strike zone."

"That doesn't sound good."

"It wasn't. And to make matters worse, we barely have enough to field a team, so if we put someone in to pitch, we have to leave another position vacant."

"But I haven't pitched for a long time," I replied.

"All of the older players on our team were talking about how good you were. They said you put a beautiful spin on the ball and made it drop through the strike zone at the last second, causing the batter to strike and miss."

I had been quite good when I was younger. We had played in the championship multiple times with me as pitcher. But I finally had to give up softball. As my family grew, so did the time commitment I needed for them. I considered his request and realized with my children mostly grown, I could probably try my hand at softball again. But would I be able to pitch like I used to?

"I'm willing to give it a try," I said. "But I'd like to practice."

"We won't be practicing again before the game tomorrow,"

Mel replied. "But if you want to come early, I'd be happy to catch for you."

That was the best we could do, so we agreed to meet an hour early. As we practiced, I was disappointed in my skills. Only about fifty percent of the balls dropped through the strike zone. If I tried to put on my old spin, my success fell to about thirty percent. When I mentioned my inadequate percentages, my neighbor encouraged me.

"It's better than anyone did last night."

When the game started, the other team won the toss and took the field first. I only got one chance to hit in the first inning, and I popped a ball to center for our first out. We didn't score at all.

We moved to the field, and I went to pitch. I walked the first three batters. My team called out encouragement, but I could tell they were frustrated with me. The fourth batter caught my pitch and drilled the ball right back at me. It hit me in the forehead, and I flipped onto my back, hitting my head on the ground. My team was able to stop the last two runners after two had scored. Then they gathered around as I lay on the ground.

"We're all friends," Mel said to me. "You can swear if you want."

"He's too religious to swear," Rob said. Then he asked, "Daris, do you want me to swear for you?"

They were concerned that I couldn't continue, but I knew they were counting on me, so I pulled myself to my feet. I swayed a little but eventually stood steady. Everyone moved back to their positions.

The next batter was one of the other team's best, and he pounded the plate with his bat, grinning at me. I threw a beautiful pitch with a perfect spin. He struck and missed. There were two more beautiful pitches and two more strikes. I struck out the next two batters as well. From that point, I pitched an almost flawless game. I struck out more than half of the other team's batters, and those who did hit popped the ball to an immediate out. We won six to two.

As the team gathered around to congratulate me after our win, Rob said, "Next time Daris pitches for us, let's just hit him in the head to start with so he pitches perfectly right from the start."

114

High Steak Deals

✦

My scouts, like most young boys, were very competitive and always looking for an edge on everything. That seemed especially true when it came to food. They always wanted the biggest cookie, the best-looking cupcake, or the largest steak.

I had only been a scoutmaster for a short time when I first saw this. The boys had earned a few merit badges, and we were having a court of honor. I had asked the parents to rotate on who brought treats to our events. It was Mort's mother's turn, and she was a good cook. Even before the court of honor had started, the boys were eyeing the beautiful cupcakes, each boy deciding which one he wanted. With only one cupcake apiece, I knew what would happen when the court of honor was over—the boys would make a mad dash for the dessert table in hopes of getting the one each desired. But Gordy had an idea on how to get a jump on the rush.

As the boys were gathered around the table, Gordy separated out the cupcake he wanted, the biggest one with the most icing and sprinkles. He made sure he had the attention of all the other boys.

Once he knew they were watching, he said, "This is the one I want," and stuck his finger in the middle of it.

"That's not fair," Mort said.

"Why?" Gordy replied, grinning. "Someone else can choose it if they want to."

"Not after you stuck your filthy finger in it," Mort said.

I could see that the others agreed with Mort and felt it was unfair. Cupcakes are important to young scouts, so I thought I should do something. But what? Suddenly I had an idea. I don't know if it was a good idea, but I felt it might teach the boys something about fairness and not being greedy.

"I agree with Gordy," I said, sticking my finger into the cupcake Gordy had claimed. "I think we should go ahead and let him have this one."

"Hey!" Gordy protested as I licked the icing off my finger.

About half of the boys followed suit, agreeing that the cupcake was Gordy's as they stuck their fingers into it. The rest would have done likewise, but Gordy protected what was left of his designated cupcake. Most of the icing was gone, licked off many fingers, and the cake itself was just crumbs.

I thought Gordy had learned his lesson, but it was on our next month's campout when I learned otherwise. We had almost one steak per person. I say almost because there were sixteen boys and two leaders, but only seventeen steaks. One steak was the size of two others, so we had just planned to cut it in half.

We had just finished cooking all the steaks and were preparing to eat, but before I had a chance to cut the big one in half, Gordy stopped me. Just like with the cupcake, he made sure everyone was looking, and then he spit on the big steak.

He grinned and said, "If no one wants that steak I'd be happy to eat it."

I could feel the annoyance welling up in me, but before I could say anything, Mort walked up and spit on the steak Gordy had just claimed.

"Yeah, Gordy, it's all yours," he said.

The boys who were closest followed Mort's example. Gordy was faster in protecting the steak than he had been the cupcake, and only five of the boys were able to help him mark it as his own. But in trying to protect the steak, he knocked it off the table into the dirt.

Gordy wanted to choose another steak, but I said because of him there wasn't even one for me, and there was only one apiece for everyone else. He took the big steak and tried to wash it off. We reheated it to burn off the contamination, but he still claimed it had grit in it.

I couldn't help but rub it in a little. "Maybe that's what greed tastes like," I told him.

Girls' Camp Bears

✦

I took my daughter to meet up with her group with her carpool group for girls' camp. It was early in the morning, and I stayed while the leaders gave last-minute instructions.

"And don't forget," the head leader said, "if you hear the bear horn, you are to get into the nearest cabin immediately."

"Yeah," a young teenaged, junior leader named Lindy added. "You will be safe there."

Lindy was a senior and fairly typical of the country girls in our community. She was athletic and pretty, and although she was quite strong, she was still feminine. I couldn't help but smile seeing her with her long blonde hair and her backwoods camping gear around her.

I also laughed to myself at the thought of the bear alarm. I could remember the fire alarm drills all those years in grade school. If it went off, everyone was to get out of the building quickly and safely. But if the bear alarm goes off, everyone is to get inside.

My daughter went off with her group, and I returned home to pack for my trip with the scouts to climb Mount Borah. We each had our own exciting week, and when I returned sweaty, tired, and with blistered feet, I looked forward to hearing about my daughter's adventures at girls' camp.

But when I walked into the house, it was quiet. "Where's Elli?" I asked my wife, Donna.

She smiled. "Where else? She's sleeping. I don't think those girls at girls' camp ever go to bed."

I watered the yard and garden and completed some other chores that needed to be done. I worked for quite a few hours before finally coming in for the evening.

"Where's Elli?" I asked.

"She still asleep," Donna replied. "But I think we should wake her up, or she won't sleep tonight."

I looked at the time—eight o'clock.

"That makes a lot of sense," I chuckled. "Let's wake her so she can go back to sleep."

We eventually woke Elli so she could eat dinner.

"How did girls' camp go?" I asked. "Did you have any bear problems?"

She nodded. "We were just finishing up dinner on the first evening when the bear alarm went off. We all rushed into the cabin. Then we gathered around in a group, and everyone told the scariest bear stories they knew."

"I bet that was fun," I said.

"Yes," she replied. "But some of the girls started to get really scared and said we should change the subject. So we quit talking, and everyone was quiet while we tried to think of something else to talk about. That's when we heard it."

"Heard what?" I asked.

"The bear," she replied. "It sounded like it was snorting. It was loud and frightening and sounded like it was almost right by us. But the scariest part was that it wasn't coming from outside. It was coming from inside the cabin."

"What did you do?" I asked.

"Well, some of the girls started to scream. Others were yelling that we should run out of the cabin, but rules said we couldn't until the all-clear was sounded. We didn't know what to do. But then one of the older girls finally calmed everyone, saying it wasn't a bear. Then she pointed at sleeping Lindy and said, 'That's the way Lindy snores.'"

I laughed, thinking of sweet, pretty, feminine Lindy snoring so loud the girls thought it was a bear.

"But," Elli said, "the worst part was that we didn't get any sleep listening to the same snoring bear every night."

Don't Mess with Mom

✦

Mary was proud of her son Richard. He was nineteen and at that time in life when most young men would be earning money, buying cars, and dating girls. But he chose to serve as a missionary in South America. He was going to be working in some areas of great poverty and would be helping the people learn to take care of themselves and to better their circumstances.

But Mary also worried about Richard. There had been hurricanes and other natural disasters where he was going, as well as disease and food shortages. Living conditions there would be hard. As she hugged him goodbye, she promised to send him packages to encourage him and to help him remember her love.

Richard hadn't even been gone a day before Mary mailed off the first care package. She packed it with cookies and letters of encouragement. The next week she mailed a package and a letter on different days so Richard would receive them at different times. Mary also emailed him on the one day each week he had email access. That became the norm from then on. But when she received emails back from Richard, it didn't take long for Mary to realize that her letters were arriving but the packages were not. And Richard said the letters were even arriving opened.

Mary contemplated what she could do. She contacted those who were in charge of the missionary efforts there and was told that a flight went down once per month to deliver packages directly to the missionaries and to carry supplies for the humanitarian effort. She could safely send packages for Richard on it. The monthly deliveries were discouraging to Mary; she had hoped to send a package every week for her son, with extra ones for special occasions.

When she heard that a big storm was coming to Richard's area, Mary decided she couldn't wait for the flight and had to try again. She packaged up a box that included warm clothes for Richard. In an effort to ensure the safe arrival of her package, she appliquéd Richard's name in blazing white letters on the warm red sweater she packed for him. She hoped that would deter the thief.

The storm hit, and Mary hoped and prayed that her son received his package. She anxiously awaited the next email and was upset to find out the package had never arrived. At least, it hadn't arrived to Richard. He said that the postmaster was wearing a beautiful red sweater with the name "Richard" as big as life on it. It obviously meant nothing to the postmaster, who knew no English.

Mary was furious. She was determined to do something, especially when Richard wrote that the postmaster made more money than anyone else in town because of his position. That made Mary maddest of all. Richard had given up other things he wanted to do in life to help people living in poverty, and the one man in town who needed it least was stealing Richard's packages.

Mary thought for a long time and finally contrived a plan that she thought might give a little justice. She once more created a special package and mailed it to Richard. When Mary finally received an email from Richard asking about something he had seen, she knew her plan had worked.

Richard's email said, "Mom, the postmaster thought he was popular because all of the American tourists wanted selfies with him to post online. He thought it was because of the new, beautiful clothes he was wearing. He didn't realize the words on them said things like 'I stole this from a missionary' and 'I'm a thief.' It has created quite a stir. The government is even looking into action against him. I can't imagine where he might have gotten clothes like that. :)"

But Richard's next line was the best. He simply said, "Maybe he'll learn it isn't good to mess with a mother's love."

Fan Club Horse Sense

✦

We were at a community reception for donors of the college arts programs. The reception was to be followed by a big summer concert. I was visiting with a friend when my wife, Donna, brought a lady over to meet me.

"This is my husband," Donna said, pointing to me. "Daris, this is Melva. She wants to meet you."

I reached out my hand. "Glad to meet you, Melva."

Melva was about sixty years old. She was a pleasant-looking woman with a big smile. She seemed almost giddy.

She took my hand and shook it. "I've got to tell you, I am one of your biggest fans. In fact, probably the only fan bigger than myself is my husband. We both race to get the paper on Thursdays so we can be first to read your story."

I smiled. "I'm glad to know that someone reads what I write. Sometimes I think my whole audience consists of my wife, my children, and birds who read the papers people use to line the bottoms of their cages."

Melva laughed. "You're funny. I do hope you'll be here for a little while. My husband should be back in about a half hour. He dropped me off and left to run some errands. He would love to meet you."

I wasn't sure how soon we planned to take our seats for the concert, so I looked at Donna. She nodded, so I knew she felt we could wait.

"Sure," I said to Melva. "We'll be around for a while."

Melva went off to keep an eye out for her husband, and Donna and I mingled with other guests. We had been involved in theatre and music for many years, and Donna was on the university committee for promotion of the arts, so we knew a lot of the people there. We enjoyed visiting, but as the time for the concert grew closer, I became concerned that we would not get very good seats.

Melva kept coming back to check and see if we were still there, and when she saw we were, she would go off again to look for her husband. Finally, just as we were ready to go to the concert hall, Melva came, in pulling a man by the hand.

"Merve," Melva said triumphantly, "guess who this is."

Merve looked completely out of place at such a formal event. All of the women were wearing dresses, most of the men were wearing suits, and the men not in suits were wearing collared shirts and ties. That is, all except for Merve. He wore a nice flannel shirt, new blue jeans, cowboy boots, a polo tie, and an expression that said he'd rather be almost anywhere else.

"How am I supposed to know?" he asked Melva.

"Think of your favorite things to do every week," Melva said.

Merve thought a minute. He then looked at me and asked, "Do you work at the feed store?"

I laughed, and Melva said, "No, Merve. Think of the newspaper."

Suddenly it dawned on him who I was. "Why, you're Mr. Howard, aren't you?" I nodded, and he grabbed my hand and shook it heartily. "You don't look anything like your picture in the paper, but then I'm sure they did that Photoshop stuff to make it look better than real."

I wasn't quite sure what to say. I knew no one had Photoshopped it.

"When I read your story about the farm and ranch store," Merve said, "I laughed so hard I almost broke a rib. In fact, I named one of my horses after you."

"Really?" I said. "That's quite an honor. I'd like to see your horse."

"Sorry," Merve said. "Can't do that. He was the stupidest

animal I ever owned, and I finally had to sell him."

I guess my fan club is down one horse.

If you enjoyed our book, we would love to have you do a review on Amazon at: http://amzn.com/1629860174

Would you like to see *Life's Outtakes* column running in your local paper or magazine? Suggest it to the editor. If an editor runs the *Life's Outtakes* column due to your suggestion, we will send you a free autographed book by Daris Howard. Find out more at:
http://www.darishoward.com

Read stories, purchase books, or subscribe to our short story list by going to:
http://www.publishinginspiration.com

Daris Howard's Amazon page:
http://amzn.com/e/B004H76UGK

For inspiring plays and books, as well as discounts for booksellers, go to

http://www.publishinginspiration.com

About the Author

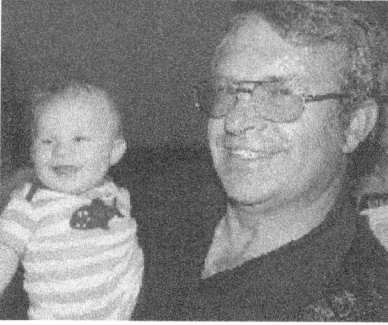

Daris Howard, an award winning author and playwright, grew up on an Idaho farm. He was a state champion athlete, competed in college athletics, and lived for a time in New York.

He has worked as a cowboy, a mechanic, in farming, and in the timber industry. He is now a college professor. He has also been a scoutmaster, having up to 18 boys in his scout troop at a time. In his wide range of experience, he has associated with many colorful characters who form a basis for his writing. Daris has had plays translated into German and French, and his plays have been performed in many countries around the world. For many years Daris has written a popular column called *Life's Outtakes* that consists of weekly short stories, and is published in various newspapers and magazines in the U.S. and Canada.

www.ingramcontent.com/pod-product-compliance
Lightning Source LLC
Chambersburg PA
CBHW061738020426
42331CB00006B/1286